Cambridge Elements

Elements in Business Strategy
edited by
J.-C. Spender
Kozminski University

DYNAMIC CAPABILITIES: FOUNDATIONAL CONCEPTS

David J. Teece
University of California, Berkeley

Shaftesbury Road, Cambridge CB2 8EA, United Kingdom

One Liberty Plaza, 20th Floor, New York, NY 10006, USA

477 Williamstown Road, Port Melbourne, VIC 3207, Australia

314–321, 3rd Floor, Plot 3, Splendor Forum, Jasola District Centre, New Delhi – 110025, India

103 Penang Road, #05-06/07, Visioncrest Commercial, Singapore 238467

Cambridge University Press is part of Cambridge University Press & Assessment, a department of the University of Cambridge.

We share the University's mission to contribute to society through the pursuit of education, learning and research at the highest international levels of excellence.

www.cambridge.org
Information on this title: www.cambridge.org/9781009562751
DOI: 10.1017/9781009562713

© David J. Teece 2025

This publication is in copyright. Subject to statutory exception and to the provisions of relevant collective licensing agreements, with the exception of the Creative Commons version the link for which is provided below, no reproduction of any part may take place without the written permission of Cambridge University Press & Assessment.

An online version of this work is published at doi.org/10.1017/9781009562713 under a Creative Commons Open Access license CC-BY-NC 4.0 which permits re-use, distribution and reproduction in any medium for non-commercial purposes providing appropriate credit to the original work is given and any changes made are indicated. To view a copy of this license visit https://creativecommons.org/licenses/by-nc/4.0

When citing this work, please include a reference to the DOI 10.1017/9781009562713

First published 2025

A catalogue record for this publication is available from the British Library

ISBN 978-1-009-56275-1 Hardback
ISBN 978-1-009-56274-4 Paperback
ISSN 2515-0693 (online)
ISSN 2515-0685 (print)

Cambridge University Press & Assessment has no responsibility for the persistence or accuracy of URLs for external or third-party internet websites referred to in this publication and does not guarantee that any content on such websites is, or will remain, accurate or appropriate.

For EU product safety concerns, contact us at Calle de José Abascal, 56, 1°, 28003 Madrid, Spain, or email eugpsr@cambridge.org

Dynamic Capabilities: Foundational Concepts

Elements in Business Strategy

DOI: 10.1017/9781009562713
First published online: June 2025

David J. Teece
University of California, Berkeley

Author for correspondence: David J. Teece, dteece@thinkbrg.com

Abstract: The dynamic capabilities framework outlines the means by which the managers of business enterprises foster and exercise organizational and technological capabilities and business strategy to address current and anticipated market and geopolitical conditions. In a firm with strong dynamic capabilities, managers can establish and periodically renew the competitive advantage of the business enterprise by not just responding to but shaping the business environment. This Element relates the dynamic capabilities framework to important concepts from the business and economics literature, demonstrating how it applies to today's business challenges. It also offers a capabilities perspective on a theory of the firm. Most existing theories of the firm caricature today's business enterprise. For advanced students of business, this Element provides a deeper understanding of the dynamic capabilities framework. For managers and boards, it shows how the analytical tools and mindsets that help to make their firms future-ready can be better understood in terms of the dynamic capabilities framework. This Element is also available as Open Access on Cambridge Core.

This Element also has a video abstract: http://www.cambridge.org/EBUS_TeeceJ_abstract

Keywords: competitive advantage, dynamic capabilities, entrepreneurial management, innovation, strategy

© David J. Teece 2025

ISBNs: 9781009562751 (HB), 9781009562744 (PB), 9781009562713 (OC)
ISSNs: 2515-0693 (online), 2515-0685 (print)

Contents

Introduction | 1

1 Capabilities: An Introduction | 1

2 Dynamic Capabilities: Some Foundational Concepts | 8

3 The Economic Theory of the Firm | 36

4 Building a Capabilities Theory of the Firm | 44

5 Conclusions | 63

References | 65

Introduction

The field of strategic management analyzes the science and art of making the key decisions that drive the successes, failures, and futures of firms large and small. A relatively recent but widely accepted framework in strategic management is that of dynamic capabilities. These capabilities determine a firm's ability to create, find, and exploit opportunities while maintaining external and internal alignment as the business environment evolves. The dynamic capabilities framework is described at length in a companion Element in this series: *Dynamic Capabilities and Related Paradigms*. That Element also compares the dynamic capabilities approach to other perspectives on innovation and strategy.

In this Element, I will briefly recap the dynamic capabilities framework before tackling two more specialized topics that cover some of the intellectual foundations on which the dynamic capabilities framework rests. The first of these is a review of significant concepts from business and economics that preceded – and, in a few cases, influenced – the development of the dynamic capabilities framework. Such concepts are typically spread across business curricula with no real attempt at integration. Here, I present their conceptual interconnections with the dynamic capabilities framework. The second main section concerns a set of more fundamental microeconomic concepts collectively known as the theory of the firm. The leading economic theories of the firm, adopted by many economics and business scholars, are influential in the formulation of public policy and regulation, but they are narrowly drawn constructs that bear little relationship to how actual firms operate. The capabilities perspective presents an opportunity to develop a much richer – and more realistic – theory of the firm.

1 Capabilities: An Introduction

I firmly believe that one cannot adequately explain the wealth of either firms or nations without a theory of organizational capabilities. Most policy makers and many businesspeople view wealth creation through the lens of economics. It is true that, in a market economy, the allocation of resources is guided by the "invisible hand" of the price system. This ignores, though, the massive amount of allocation done within large firms, where prices may not be determinative, which enables managers, under the supervision of boards of directors, to make resource allocation decisions.

In the microeconomic textbook view, firms combine (generic) labor, "capital," and technology to produce products and services. Allocation of factors of production takes place more or less automatically, guided by the relative prices of factor inputs. Cost differences among firms can occur, but, in many applications, all firms are assumed to be using the most efficient combination of various factors of production.

In the real world, workers aren't homogeneous units of labor. They have different skill sets and need to be motivated and guided. Incentives matter, but so do corporate culture and leadership. Nor are machines simply interchangeable units of capital. They have different vintages and qualities. Technology, of course, can also vary widely across firms, in part because they have different histories and strategies. Organizational structure matters, too. The goods and services that firms produce vary in quality and features. Firms also differ in the mix of products and services each one opts to produce. Productivity varies markedly amongst firms in the same industry. In short, heterogeneity, not homogeneity, is the norm. There is no such thing as the "representative firm" that economic theory commonly assumes to exist.

Some of these distinctions can be – and have been – mentioned and, sometimes, modeled by economists when it suits their proclivities. But there is a deeper type of difference to which economists have turned a blind eye: the organizational capabilities that each firm brings to bear as its managers make (strategic) investment choices. Studies have shown, for example, that even in mature industries, the productivity of factories producing similar products can vary significantly due to the ways in which managers decide to operate (Bloom et al., 2012).

While management research makes extensive use of economic methods, economics favors a black-box model of the firm at the micro level, although there are occasional attempts to open the black box. The capabilities and histories of business enterprises, including past strategic and operational decisions of their managers, are arguably the main drivers of inter-firm differences in financial performance. These considerations are usually missing from economic models.

Somewhat surprisingly, it is only in the present century that managers have been acknowledged as a legitimate subject for economic research, and such studies are still rare. In an early example, economists Bertrand and Schoar (2003) researched a sample of about 500 C-level executives who had moved from one major US company to another and found significant manager-related effects in return on assets as well as in a number of operating variables such as acquisition activity. Another study in this vein, by Acemoglu, Akcigit, and Celik (2022), looked at the relation of corporate culture to radical (as opposed to incremental) innovation. One of their variables is the average age of the firms' top managers, and they found a small but significant inverse relation between manager age and radical innovation. In short, economists have belatedly "discovered" that individual managerial identities matter. This is hardly a surprise to the population at large; but it has had a hard time entering the economic theories that frequently influence regulations, laws, and judicial opinions.

The capabilities view of the firm to be outlined in this section looks beyond factors of production and firms' production functions to recognize the importance of the past and present choices of managers to generate and allocate financial and human resources. It also recognizes that technology and know-how do not fall like manna from heaven but rather result from search and investment. In this way, the capabilities view can help explain interfirm heterogeneity, enterprise evolution, and organizational longevity – topics of great importance to the economic theory of the firm.

1.1 Resources versus Capabilities

A related term commonly used in the strategic management literature is resources. These are the tangible and intangible assets, broadly defined, that the firm can develop and effectively manage and control. Resources, which include the skills of the firm's employees, its equipment, and the collective skills of the organization, generate streams of services that the firm can deploy. "Resources" in strategic management are akin to "factors of production" in economics, but they are more granular. While economic models generally assume factors of production are deployed on the efficiency frontier, strategic management theories recognize that the manner in which a firm's resources are coordinated and managed is at least as important to competitive success and survival as the identity of the resources themselves.

Capabilities such as an ability to spot new opportunities and create new markets are vital to profitable resource management. They are embedded in the knowledge and routines of top, middle, and lower-down employees and reflect the way they work together. Capabilities matter even more with the internet and the spread of digital technology.

Capabilities arise in part from learning (including the conduct of R&D), from combining resources, and from experience with using complementary assets. Many capabilities become implanted in organizational routines. Others reside with the top management team.

Organizational capabilities can usefully be thought of as falling into one of two interconnected (but analytically separable) categories: ordinary (and superordinary) capabilities and dynamic capabilities. Ordinary (and superordinary) capabilities are to a large extent operational, determining how a firm functions at a point in time. Dynamic capabilities are generally strategic in nature, relate to how physical and financial assets are deployed, and play a large role in determining how profitable the firm will be in the future.

Capabilities are not appropriately summarized by the "production functions" in economic models because capabilities are untethered from particular product outputs.[1] For example, a capability to make machines powered by small, compact internal combustion engines can manifest itself in the manufacturing of motorcycles, outboard (boat) motors, or lawn mowers. Other capabilities, such as the ability to offer outstanding customer service, may not be tied to a single product area at all.

A higher-level category of capability was posited by Teece, Pisano, and Shuen in a 1990 working paper (revised and published in 1997). These "dynamic capabilities" (Teece, Pisano, and Shuen, 1990) are integral to selecting, developing, and coordinating assets and ordinary capabilities.

The dynamic capabilities framework has become one of the leading perspectives on the firm in the field of strategic management (Di Stefano, Peteraf, and Verona, 2010). It seeks to explain a monumentally important phenomenon – firm survival (or failure) and long-run growth and prosperity – by detailing how firms can create, extend, integrate, modify, and deploy their resources while simultaneously managing competitive threats and effectuating necessary transformations (Teece, 2010a).

1.2 A Capabilities Taxonomy

All capabilities involve some mix of organizational routines and management's decision-making acumen. A fundamental distinction is the difference between ordinary capabilities (predominantly routine) and dynamic capabilities (largely reliant on managerial decisions). Ordinary (and superordinary) capabilities are how the organization converts its resources into products and services within its current business model. Dynamic capabilities are how the firm determines the resources (including capabilities) and business model(s) it needs for the future. There are gradations within both these categories, to the details of which we now turn.

1.2.1 Ordinary (and Superordinary) Capabilities

Ordinary capabilities, which encompass operations, administration, and governance of the firm's activities, allow the firm to produce and sell a defined set of products and services. Ordinary capabilities are embedded in some combination of (1) skilled personnel, including, under certain circumstances, independent contractors; (2) facilities and equipment; (3) processes and routines, including any supporting technical manuals; and (4) the administrative coordination needed to get the job done.

---

[1] In economics, a production function specifies the technical relation between efficient combinations of inputs, such as land, labor, and machines, and the resulting quantities of output.

A firm's ordinary capabilities support technical efficiency (and hence productivity) in performing a fixed group of activities, regardless of how well- or ill-suited the outputs are to the market's competitive needs (Teece, 2007). Quality control methodologies, performance measurement, and payroll execution are examples of ordinary capabilities. The corresponding managerial modes include cost control and (static) optimization.

Ordinary capabilities can be measured against the requirements of specific tasks, such as labor productivity, inventory turns, and time to completion, and can thus be benchmarked internally or externally to industry best practices. The process of measuring and benchmarking increases the likelihood that the benchmarked capabilities can be bought or imitated by rivals using consultants and other available knowledge sources. Because of this imitability, good ordinary capabilities are generally insufficient to ensure a firm's success and survival. While the diffusion of best practices is clearly neither instant nor complete, it takes only a few firms at the frontier to drive prices down to competitive levels, thereby dissipating any economic rents (profits above the level required to cover costs). The insufficiency of ordinary capabilities is most obvious after market demand shifts; there is no benefit to being very good at delivering products for which market demand has evaporated.

The development of excellence in performing a set of ordinary capabilities can actually lead a firm into complacency; a single-minded pursuit of efficiency and productivity can drive out the willingness to effectuate change when market conditions change. Henry Ford learned this the hard way a century ago. His Ford Motor Company used vertical integration to optimize the production process for the Model T. This worked well until the market shifted. Bringing a follow-on product, the Model A, to market was a long and arduous process that allowed General Motors (GM) to get ahead of Ford, a leadership position GM held for decades. As Benner and Tushman noted: "Activities focused on measurable efficiency and variance reduction drive out variance-increasing activities and, thus, affect an organization's ability to innovate and adapt outside of existing trajectories … Core capabilities may become core rigidities" (Benner and Tushman, 2003, p. 242).

In certain cases, excellence in an organization's ordinary capabilities can overcome the limitations of routines and become a source of prolonged advantage, particularly in sectors where technology is relatively stable. These "super-ordinary" capabilities are a form of "signature process" (Gratton and Ghoshal, 2005), a valuable set of routines that have evolved in unique and nonobvious ways, which in turn makes them hard for others to imitate. Even signature processes will become imitable or beatable by others over time, but it could be a long time, even decades, depending on the levels of competition and market turbulence. The achievement of superordinary capabilities by some firms and not others helps to explain the wide dispersion of productivity within an industry among firms making more or less the same suite of products and services. However, even superordinary capabilities may become far less valuable after the market shifts, as seen during the transition from internal combustion engines to electric vehicles.

1.2.2 Dynamic Capabilities

Unlike ordinary capabilities, dynamic capabilities are hard for rivals to imitate or emulate because they rely more heavily on the entrepreneurial spirit, cognition, and attitude toward risk of the top management team. Under deep uncertainty (see Section 2.1.1), two organizations may receive the same set of market signals, yet draw opposite conclusions about, for instance, whether a new subscription model for an existing pay-as-you-go service would generate sufficient revenue to justify making the change.

Dynamic capabilities help enable an enterprise to profitably build and renew resources, reconfiguring them as needed to innovate and respond to (or bring about) changes in the market and in the business environment more generally (Pisano and Teece, 2007; Teece, Pisano, and Shuen, 1997). Strong dynamic capabilities allow the enterprise and its top management to develop conjectures about the evolution of consumer preferences, business problems, and technology; validate and fine-tune them; and then act on them by realigning assets and activities. Such capabilities are necessary and valuable when deep uncertainty is present, requiring managers to respond well to novel situations, such as a global pandemic, that may not have occurred for a long time, if ever. Firms also have lower-order dynamic capabilities. These are activities that entail the reconfiguration of resources but which the firm performs repeatedly so that there is a larger role for routines. These include activities such as acquisitions and new product development. Strong dynamic capabilities support innovation and high performance and rely on a change-oriented organizational culture and prescient assessments of the business environment and technological opportunities by the top management team.

Although, for discussion purposes, it is simplest to talk about dynamic capabilities as a collective object, it is important to bear in mind that they consist of many different activities, the roster of which will vary somewhat between firms. Each activity potentially demands managerial attention and, possibly, investment, to remain fine-tuned. In some business environments, such as those where technology is stable, where firms are heavily regulated, or where markets are closed to new entrants, the payoff from developing strong dynamic capabilities may not be high. In general, a given firm will be weaker in some dynamic capabilities than others for any number of reasons. However, weak dynamic capabilities will undermine the firm's overall performance when operating in environments characterized by deep uncertainty and other sources of turbulence. To describe the contemporary business environment, it is not uncommon for businesspeople to refer to VUCA, a military acronym that stands for volatility, uncertainty, complexity, and ambiguity.

To bring some specificity to this subject, high-order dynamic capabilities can usefully be broken down into three primary clusters: (1) identification and assessment of threats, opportunities, and customer needs (*sensing*); (2) mobilization of resources to address fresh opportunities while capturing value from doing so (*seizing*); and (3) ongoing organizational renewal (*transforming*). These activities are required to create and sustain a firm's competitive advantage. They need not be performed sequentially, often taking place in parallel on a more or less ongoing basis. Engagement in continuous or semi-continuous sensing, seizing, and transforming is essential if the firm is to sustain its performance as customers, competitors, and technologies change (Teece, 2007).

While the decisions of individual managers and the top management team play a large role in a firm's dynamic capabilities, the organization's embedded values and culture as well as its collective ability and willingness to change are also integral (Teece, 2010b). The organizational aspects of dynamic capabilities are the product of past managerial decisions and current managerial leadership but that makes them slow to change, complex to understand, and difficult to imitate. Unlike ordinary capabilities, dynamic capabilities can't easily be outsourced or acquired; they must often be "built" and maintained through investments of time and resources in discovery, knowledge generation, and learning. Sometimes, a small acquisition can create a beachhead upon which a larger organization can rapidly scale; recognizing the opportunity and effectuating it well requires strong dynamic capabilities.

Strong dynamic capabilities are necessary to determine whether the current slate of products and services will be the right path to follow in the future. Ordinary capabilities, by contrast, are valuable only during a given market window. It is only dynamic capabilities that can provide a firm the potential to sustain competitive advantage as the business environment changes.

1.3 Dynamic Capabilities and Strategy

Dynamic capabilities encompass the activities that constitute the core elements of strategic management. They allow managers to determine where the organization needs to go and the resources and investments required to get there. A big exception is the formulation of strategy itself, the determination of how the firm's managers will solve the puzzle(s) posed by the meeting of its business model with market demand, technological change, and the general business environment.

The analytic split between dynamic capabilities and strategy, while perhaps surprising, is natural because dynamic capabilities are cultivated over time and adaptable to a variety of contexts whereas a good strategy is context-specific. Dynamic capabilities guide decisions such as which strategy to pursue, including the R&D programs to support, which products and services to make, and which customers to target. Strategy determines the timing of market entry, the manner of entry, and how to serve customers while keeping competitors at bay.

While we can think of dynamic capabilities and strategy as analytically distinct, the division between them is less clear in practice, not least because top management bears responsibility for both.

A good strategy starts from a sound diagnosis of the focal challenge. The diagnosis informs the development and adoption of a guiding policy approach to address the challenge. The policy then becomes the springboard for devising and implementing a plan of coherent action (Rumelt, 2011). Clearly, this sequence entails some exercise of the firm's dynamic capabilities. Diagnosis, for example, requires sensing to assess the internal and external parameters of the strategy. Undertaking a program of coherent action to implement a strategy will likely call on the firm's seizing capabilities. The nature of good strategy is addressed at more length in the companion Element, *Dynamic Capabilities and Related Paradigms*.

A sound strategy is necessary in order for dynamic capabilities to be fully effective. Figure 1 provides a schematic view of the dynamic capabilities framework, indicating how capabilities and strategy codetermine performance. Firms with weaker capabilities will require different strategies than firms with stronger capabilities. And the effectiveness of dynamic capabilities would be undermined by poor strategy.

2 Dynamic Capabilities: Some Foundational Concepts

Strategic management research by scholars, management consultants, and corporations is ever-expanding in its scope. While this is generally positive, in the sense of developing ideas about competitive outcomes, it has mostly produced a long series of silver-bullet explanations for competitive advantage rather than the careful construction of an integrated theory that could prove more durable (Durand, Grant, and Madsen, 2017).

There are undoubtedly certain commonalities to the ways that successful firms in different contexts approach the challenges of creating new markets and confronting market rivalry. The dynamic capabilities framework is designed to

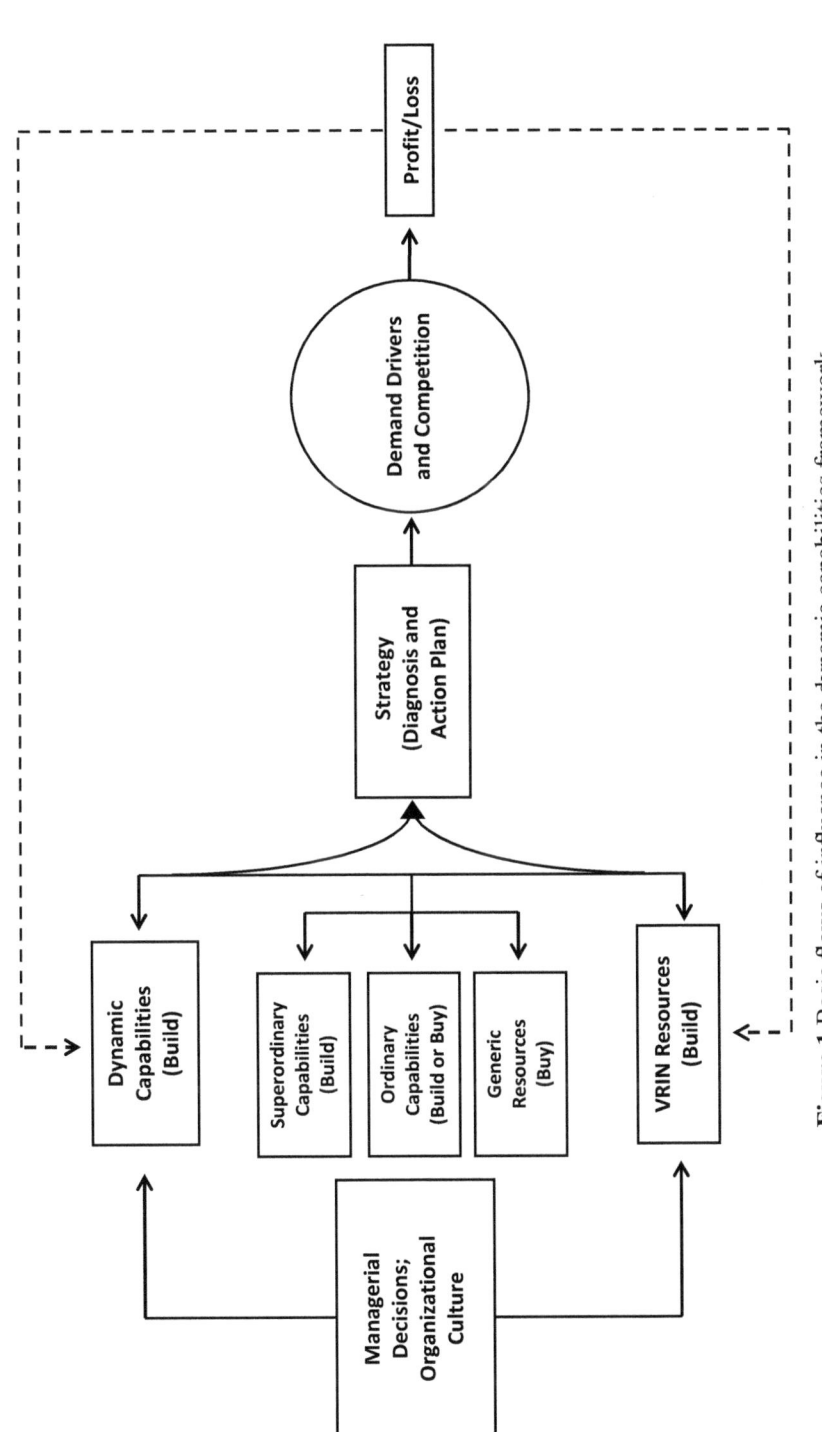

Figure 1 Basic flows of influence in the dynamic capabilities framework

highlight these commonalities, enabling it to accommodate a wide range of variables and concepts. I argued more than a decade ago that the framework can be used to integrate most topics in business within its overarching model of how individual firms pursue competitive advantage (Teece, 2011a). To demonstrate this integrative potential, this section looks at key concepts developed in economics and management studies during the twentieth century and how they are compatible with the dynamic capabilities framework.[2] I'm calling them antecedents in a temporal, but not a causal, sense. Except where stated otherwise, they did not directly contribute to the formulation of the dynamic capabilities construct. They enrich our understanding of strategic management, and it is in that sense that they are foundational to the dynamic capabilities framework.

The concepts discussed in this section are (loosely) organized in terms of the three groups of activities identified earlier. First is the sensing (and making sense) of trends, prospects, and threats. Second is the seizing of opportunities by orchestrating capabilities and other resources. And third is the transforming required to build and rebuild an agile and competitive organization. References to sensing, seizing, and transforming will be used here in order to make the linkages between dynamic capabilities and these foundational concepts explicit.

2.1 Sensing: Antecedents

Sensing threats and opportunities is a constant imperative for managers. They must do so whether the future is clear or murky. Good sensing requires using both external signals, such as consumer feedback, and internal resources, such as research and development (R&D). R&D can also drive discovery, creating opportunities which are then candidates for investing (seizing).

2.1.1 Risk versus Uncertainty

Sensing capabilities are particularly important where the business environment is characterized by deep uncertainty – uncertainty which needs to be addressed differently from risk, with which it is often confused. With risk, the manager does not know what is going to happen but knows what the probability distribution of possible outcomes looks like. The model would be something like a short-range weather forecast. With deep uncertainty, however, we don't know what is going to happen or what the possible distribution of outcomes (or

---

[2] Comparisons of the dynamic capabilities framework with overlapping approaches to strategic management and innovation can be found in a companion Element in this series, *Dynamic Capabilities and Related Paradigms*.

futures) looks like. We don't even know the range of possible outcomes. New storms never experienced before in a given geography may suddenly arise.

In a sense, business, like life, is always uncertain because unanticipated dangers can spring from anywhere. Technological uncertainty, which stems from many sources including the combinations of new components and new configurations of previously combined components, is a common feature across modern economies but is poorly understood. Most high technology industries are particularly prone to unforeseen innovations exiting stealth mode and causing a big shift in consumer demand. This is what happened with the introduction of the iPhone in 2007. Until then, few people seriously thought a handheld computer-phone was a good or practical idea. A few years later, the former leaders in the cell phone market, Nokia and RIM, were struggling to survive. This occurred not only because they failed to see how broadband networks would enable internet connections on the phone; it was also because they didn't have the software capabilities that Apple could bring to bear (Teece, 2023a).

Other aspects of the global business environment, including the political positions of whole countries, seem more subject to sudden, out-of-nowhere changes than was once the case. The fading of the US hegemonic role in a newly multipolar world is leading to much greater geopolitical uncertainty. And the interconnectedness of the global economy can propagate shockwaves from once-obscure corners of the globe to major markets in the turn of a news cycle.

The difference between risk and uncertainty was analyzed more than a century ago by economist Frank Knight. Knight (1921) explained that with uncertainty present, the primary problem for managers and investors is figuring out what to do. Execution (how to do it) is decidedly secondary. Uncertainty occasionally achieves public prominence. Nassim Taleb's 2007 book about the financial industry titled *The Black Swan* (Taleb, 2007) was a salutary reminder that not every eventually can be accounted for.

Yet the strategic management of uncertainty in business is underdeveloped. The management of risk, which can be quantified in terms of probability, is widely taught, well understood, and widely practiced. But applying risk management tools like the point forecasts required of traditional capital budgeting can be "downright dangerous" and provide false comfort (Courtney, Kirkland, & Viguerie, 1997). Of course, a large unexpected shock can also turn out to be a potential positive, too. But that will also test an organization, as when a supplier suddenly receives a large order for a new component.

Unforeseeable external changes are what Nobel Laureate Tjalling Koopmans (1957) called primary uncertainty. Managers, especially in larger organizations, also face secondary uncertainty, which arises from a lack of communication across decision-making centers within an organization or across a network of firms. Internal sensing, such as opening lines of communication among divisions or partners, can reduce the prevalence of behavioral surprises that hinder execution.

Preparing for primary uncertainty is difficult because it basically requires a company to be ready for anything, able to absorb and rapidly respond to major upheavals. The goal should be to navigate unexpected events before problems reach crisis proportions. Organizational resilience and agility are not cost-free to develop, but, for firms in turbulent or unpredictable environments, they will pay dividends in a wide range of circumstances and may even spell the difference between survival and bankruptcy. The degree of flexibility must align with the firm's (context-derived) strategy.

Flexibility is largely a matter of organizational culture, incentives, and leadership (Hitt, Keats, and DeMarie, 1998). To some extent, though, it can be obtained through investment choices. As Netflix CEO Reed Hastings observed, "at Netflix we almost always prefer to pay more for the option that gives us greater flexibility, knowing that we can't – and shouldn't – try to foresee what our business will look like down the road" (Hastings and Meyer, 2020).

Strong dynamic capabilities aid in dealing with uncertainty through sensing and sensemaking exercises (Teece, Peteraf, and Leih, 2016). Sensing under uncertainty is both more difficult and more vital than sensing when the environment is more certain. Logically, sensing under uncertainty may seem pointless since the uncertain is by definition unpredictable. However, as a social scientist once put it, "while we have to be prepared to be surprised by the future, we do not have to be dumbfounded" (Boulding, 1984).

2.1.2 Entrepreneurialism

Sensing capabilities are also closely associated with the idea of entrepreneurialism. To eighteenth-century thinkers such as Richard Cantillon, who is credited with the first use of "entrepreneur," an entrepreneur was someone who put capital at risk to bring together factors of production needed to implement a money-making idea (Pesciarelli, 1988). This captured one type of combination that entrepreneurs bring about, but it was perhaps not until Schumpeter (1934) that the idea of "new combinations" of ideas, equipment, markets, and more was conceptualized as the essence of entrepreneurialism – and of economic growth.

There is of course more to entrepreneurialism than just recognizing promising new combinations. First, there is the process of sifting through the countless potential combinations that exist. Each must be calibrated in terms of the size of the addressable market, technological feasibility, and commercial viability in order to identify the best investment opportunity. Next, an organization must be built or reshaped to meet the requirements of the new activities. As new capabilities are developed and investments made, resources must be coordinated and kept in alignment.

These activities seem – and in fact are – very similar to the sensing, seizing, and transforming activities of the dynamic capabilities framework (Augier and Teece, 2009; Teece, 2012a). Entrepreneurial management, which also includes the leadership necessary to inspire and motivate an organization, is the heart of the organization's dynamic capabilities (Schoemaker, Heaton, and Teece, 2018; Teece, 2016a). The more entrepreneurial and empowered the firm's employees are, the better. Netflix CEO Reed Hastings described it as the difference between a classical orchestra and a jazz ensemble:

> During the industrial era, many of the best companies operated like symphonic orchestras, with synchronicity, precision, and perfect coordination as the goal. With the growth in importance of intellectual property ... [t]he objective is no longer error prevention and replicability ... it's creativity and agility. The biggest risk isn't making a mistake ... it's failing to attract top talent, to invent new products, or to change direction quickly when the environment shifts. Consistency and repeatability are likely to squash fresh thinking. A symphony isn't what you're going for. Build a jazz band instead .... The musicians know the overall structure of the song but have the freedom to improvise, riffing off one another, creating incredible music. (Hastings and Meyer, 2020)

To some people, "entrepreneurial management" in large organizations may sound like a contradiction in terms. Entrepreneurship is typically conceived as a phenomenon for startup firms pursuing a new idea or business concept. Increasingly, however, large organizations are learning to respond to the rapid changes that digitization has brought in ways similar to startup firms, including the quick generation of software updates, rapid exploration of new product and service possibilities, and rapid abandonment of unsuccessful ideas. That is the very essence of dynamic capabilities, and it's deeply embedded in the organizational DNA of almost all Silicon Valley firms – and of a growing number of firms worldwide.

Although the actions and pronouncements of the CEO are the most public representation of corporate entrepreneurship, entrepreneurial management in a dynamically capable organization extends deep into the management hierarchy. Middle managers must bridge between the visionary goals of top management and the chaotic realities of frontline workers in order for the vision to be realized. In this model, which Nonaka (1988) calls "middle-up-down management," middle managers lead cross-functional teams to engage in the give-and-take of knowledge creation. The task of top management in this model is to motivate and to make strategic choices based on the output from a team or from rival teams (Song, Lee, and Khanna, 2016). In this way, even major strategic shifts can originate at lower levels of management, as in the well documented example of Intel's exit from memory chips in the 1980s to focus on microprocessors (Burgelman, 1994). In short, strong dynamic capabilities require managers at all levels to have – and to be able to exercise – entrepreneurial skills.

2.1.3 Complementary Technologies

The entrepreneurial identification of potential new combinations, a key form of sensing, relies on the concept of complementarities. Complementarities are present whenever two or more items are more valuable in combination than in isolation – an idea in economics that dates back more than a century (Edgeworth, 1897). The complementarity can be reciprocal, like ham and eggs – both of which are potentially enjoyable in isolation. Or it can be unilateral, like video content and display devices – the content has limited value without a display outlet. Finally, the complements can be cospecialized, meaning that they are mutually necessary, like left and right shoes.

Within organizations, it is common for intangible assets, such as ways of doing business, to become so specialized to each other that they have little value if moved individually to a different organization through, for instance, a partial acquisition. Such assets can be thought of as "non-priced" because their value is so context dependent. It is, to a large extent, the custom, or "bespoke," adaptations of particular tangible and intangible assets to one another that make the firm more than the sum of its parts – and different from a marketplace in which everything is priced according to supply and demand, especially in the digital economy (Teece, 2018b).

This principle applies to innovation as well. The essence of innovation, in the Schumpeterian sense, is new combinations. This requires the detection (and creation) of not-yet-exploited complementarities. In 1836, US inventors patented the first practical combine harvester that both cut grain and threshed the edible portion from the straw in the field, replacing a separate reaper (invented in England in 1826) and a stationary threshing machine. This brought significant reductions in labor requirements and in grain waste. Almost a century later, in 1921, the US-based Atco company added an internal combustion engine to a mechanical mower (invented in England in 1830) and achieved immediate success.

Over time, through the contributions of multiple inventors, the complementary elements united to make a combine harvester were improved in ways that make them better suited to each other and to their joint purpose. In short, the identification (sensing) and effectuation (seizing)of promising new complementarities is an important part of a firm's dynamic capabilities.

Technological complementarity occurs when the full benefit (or sometimes any benefit) of the innovation cannot be achieved until some other, complementary technology (which, on its own, has only lower value uses) has been created or re-engineered (Teece, 1986). Thomas Edison, for example, didn't invent the lightbulb and electrical generators in isolation; he conceived of them as part of a complete system that included improved generators and an electrical transmission network (Rosenberg, 1979). Likewise, the introduction of a new generation of cellular network requires new modem chips, wireless standards, and handsets that implement the technologies in order to enable value creation and capture.

Technological complementarity can pose a challenge for an innovator if the complement is created (or is owned) by a separate company and becomes a bottleneck asset (discussed below under Profiting from Innovation). One solution is to create the complement in-house; but the innovator may lack the capabilities to do so (Teece, 1986, 2006). That leaves either acquisition or partnership, depending on which is the most viable.

Technological complementarities are pervasive in the digital economy. Complicated products such as smartphones with many components and functions "read on" hundreds, if not thousands, of patents. Because of this multi-invention context, system-level innovation requires the in-licensing of patent portfolios to facilitate design and operating freedom (Grindley and Teece, 1997; Somaya and Teece, 2006). This poses distinct strategic complexities because the sources of innovation have become more widely dispersed geographically as well as organizationally.

2.1.4 Absorptive Capacity

A particular perspective on complementarity is embedded in the concept of "absorptive capacity," which was popularized by Cohen and Levinthal (1990). It focuses on the potential complementarity of internal and external knowledge. More specifically, absorptive capacity includes the ability of a firm to identify useful external knowledge, combine it with existing internal knowledge, and commercialize the result. It thus bridges sensing and seizing, at least in the realm of technology, and has itself been analyzed as a type of dynamic capability (Zahra and George, 2002).

External knowledge can exist in many forms, and firms need very different processes to interact, for instance, with a university engaged in basic research, rival firms collaborating on standards development, or suppliers involved in late-stage development work (Lim, 2009). A key unifying idea, however, is that the ability to benefit from any type of knowledge stream depends on the firm's prior internal knowledge and ability to learn (Cohen and Levinthal, 1989; Lane and Lubatkin, 1998). Thus, like other capabilities, the strength and value of a firm's absorptive capacity depend on the quality of the underlying processes and the appropriateness of the mental models used by the firm's top management and researchers.

2.1.5 General Systems Theory

To move from sensing to sensemaking, managers must adopt a big-picture perspective on the organization, its capabilities, and its environment. This calls for a system-level perspective, something which academic fields – and too many C-suite executives – fail to adopt.

The idea that the whole is more than the sum of its parts dates back to at least Aristotle's *Metaphysics* from the fourth century BC. In other words, a useful understanding of a complex system can't be obtained simply by examining its parts any more than a tail, fur, claws and whiskers could be assembled into a living cat. Understanding each of the parts is important but understanding their integration and interactions is critical because they determine the endogenous changes through which the system evolves. A holistic view is valuable at the team level, too. One of the founders of systems theory, Kenneth Boulding, noted that "one of the main objectives of General Systems Theory [is] to develop ... a framework of general theory to enable one specialist to catch relevant communications from others" (1956, p. 199).

In the case of an open system such as a corporation, general systems theory also encompasses the system's interactions with its environment. Feedback loops between the outside and the inside of the firm lead to the internal adjustments that enable adaptation to external changes while potentially shifting the external environment as well.

The development of a general theory of systems emerged in the twentieth century from separate research in various disciplines including biology, cybernetics, and economics. Economist/social scientist Kenneth Boulding made the case for a systems theory approach to management (Boulding, 1956). Systems theory became a popular approach in the 1960s and 1970s but failed to make much headway, perhaps because its early promoters, such as Boulding and C. West Churchman, failed to make it operational.

However, a systems approach to management survives in the form of a widely used congruence theory of organizational alignment by Nadler and Tushman (1980). It is still invoked at times by academics who want to emphasize the integrated nature of the elements in a model.

Systems-based approaches are difficult to implement because they are inherently cross-disciplinary, and business education currently fails to do a good job of integrating the elements of the curriculum. Academics and practitioners master fields such as accounting, marketing, operations, manufacturing, and data analytics. However, they are often unable to discuss them as integrated and interrelated activities. Yet a partial understanding of a system can impose intellectual blinders. And failure is all but guaranteed when elements of a system are mismatched. As Russell Ackoff once observed:

> Suppose you could build a dream car that included the styling of a Jaguar, the power plant of a Porsche, the suspension of a BMW, and the interior of a Rolls Royce. Put them together and what have you got? Nothing. They weren't designed to go together. They don't fit. The same is true of organizations. (Mercer LLC, 2012, p. 10)

A business model, for example, involves a product or service, a pricing logic, a geography of distribution, and so on (Teece, 2010a). These elements may or may not be chosen or developed separately from each other. However they are brought into play, the elements of the model must be coherently aligned and linked to an astute strategic vision if they are to lead to profits. If an element doesn't fit properly, for example, if productive capabilities are inadequate to reach the expected product quality and/or volume, then the model will not perform as desired.

One area where there has been at least a modest amount of systems thinking is digital platforms. The concept of indirect network effects (Clements, 2004) recognizes that a platform or service depends on two or more user groups (e.g., producers and consumers, or users and developers). As more people from one group join the platform, the platform's value to the other group increases. Companies such as Uber, Grubhub, or Facebook all rely on these indirect effects. It's not that more drivers make Uber or Lyft more valuable to other drivers (a direct effect); it's that more drivers make the service more valuable to passengers.

The study of platform business models has given rise to a recognition of the importance of business ecosystems (Jacobides, 2019; Teece, 2012b, 2016b). In ecosystems, the focus of value creation is as much outside the enterprise as within. Orchestrating relationships laterally and vertically with interdependent players requires not only strong sensing, seizing, and transforming capabilities but also a system-level perspective. The platform leader must balance its own interests with those of a plethora of actors who do not always have the same priorities, even if all of the firms share the goal of leveraging the platform.

Whereas general systems theory doesn't provide a toolkit for deciding which relationships in a digital platform or ecosystem are most critical at a particular point in time, dynamic capabilities offers guidance through its incorporation of theories such as Profiting From Innovation (discussed later). The dynamic capabilities framework (see Figure 2) is thus a workable version of systems theory for application to strategic management (Teece, 2018a), including the leadership of digital platforms and ecosystems. And, like systems theory, the dynamic capabilities approach requires interdisciplinary, ecosystem-level understanding. It demands that top managers have deep insights about many aspects of an organization and its business environment.

Many great managers follow the precepts of the dynamic capabilities framework intuitively without having the terminology to be more explicit about it. They make a change only after serious forethought about how it will play out across the organization and for all stakeholders. By making the elements and interrelationships of great management more explicit, dynamic capabilities can galvanize managers and management to allow the achievement of better results.

2.1.6 Complexity Economics

Complexity theory is the study of a particular type of system: a nonlinear dynamic system with feedback mechanisms. Complexity theory is a relatively

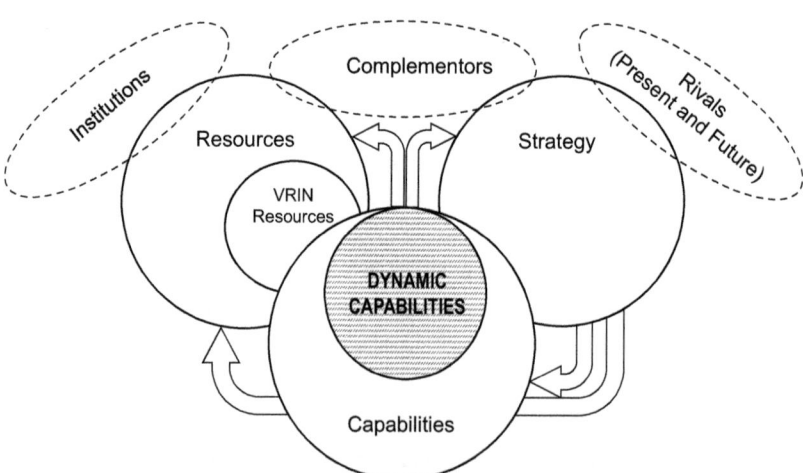

Figure 2 The key elements of the dynamic capabilities framework

Note: A dashed border indicates elements that are external to the firm. Arrows represent major interdependencies associated with the business enterprise. Markets and customers are left out; the focus here is on what economists call the supply side.

Source: Based on Teece (2018a).

young discipline that has increasingly been applied to business phenomena (Levy, 2000). It fills the gap between the broad focus of systems theory (discussed in Section 2.1.5) and the regenerative disequilibrium of inter-firm competition. For this reason, it began to attract the attention of management scholars in the 1990s.

Complex systems combine elements of systems theory with chaos theory (Schneider and Somers, 2006). Chaotic effects include unforeseen emergent properties and a tendency for small changes in key parameters to generate large changes in results. These contingent effects are in keeping with the dynamic capabilities framework's emphasis on unique, path-dependent outcomes. For example, the dynamic capabilities framework emphasizes the importance of managing complementarities among assets. In complexity terms, the combination of complementary assets can lead to the emergence of innovation not discernible from characteristics of the complements in isolation. At a higher level, the combination of the complementary sensing, seizing, and transforming activities of dynamic capabilities can lead to the emergence of superior enterprise performance (Kay, Leih, and Teece, 2018).

This is not to say that these systems are somehow predetermined. On the contrary, a theory of complex systems points to the need to develop organizational flexibility and resilience (Levy, 1994). The fundamental challenge is to find a balance between too much structure and too little, and to keep that balance aligned with the turbulence of the environment, raising the likelihood that a business can change when it needs to (Eisenhardt and Piezunka, 2011). In a study of firms in the turbulent computer industry of the 1990s, for example, Brown and Eisenhardt (1997) found that those which were most successful at innovation possessed only limited structure. This allowed for improvisation and decentralized decision making. Leaders constantly explored future scenarios to determine what new products might be needed next.

Although complexity theory is sometimes used to build formal models and generate simulations (e.g., North and Macal, 2007), the practical value of this approach is limited by the fact that, in organizations, unlike physical systems, individuals can make unpredictable changes to the "parameters" of the situation. The future, beyond a narrow window, is unknowable, and dramatic change can occur suddenly. The way forward for business enterprises, big and small, is not just to be adaptable but also to endeavor to shape the environment either through new technology or through "partnering" with regulators and governments.

The economic study of the business environment, including the behavior of consumers, investors, businesses, other populations, and institutions, is known as complexity economics. As a field, complexity economics has struggled to find its footing. It got some traction at the Santa Fe Institute, a nonprofit think tank, beginning in the late 1980s.

Complexity economics abandons the usual economic assumptions of rational actors, commonality of knowledge, and equilibrium outcomes. Instead, it views the economy as built up from individual behaviors, which react to the economy and, in turn, shape that economy, leading to new behaviors and so on, in a complex, recursive loop (Arthur, 2021).

> Complexity economics ... assumes that agents differ, that they have imperfect information about other agents and must, therefore, try to make sense of the situation they face. Agents explore, react and constantly change their actions and strategies in response to the outcome they mutually create. The resulting outcome may not be in equilibrium and may display patterns and emergent phenomena not visible to equilibrium analysis. The economy becomes something not given and existing but constantly forming from a developing set of actions, strategies and beliefs (Arthur, 2021, p. 136)

Arthur's perspective is very consistent with the dynamic capabilities framework. However, where complexity economics takes a wide-angle view and is often quite general, the dynamic capabilities approach is primarily applied at the organization level and is strongly prescriptive.

2.2 Seizing: Antecedents

After an organization settles on an innovation (whether technological or organizational) to commercialize, it relies on its seizing capabilities to develop the idea into a viable business. This involves making decisions and investments with respect to the business model(s) to be employed. To design a business model, top management must understand not just how they can generate value but how they can capture enough of that value as well. As enterprise and market interact, most business models will need to be tweaked many times because of one of the fundamental features of an innovation-driven economy: creative destruction.

2.2.1 Creative Destruction

While disruptive innovation gets a great deal of attention, not all innovation disrupts. Innovation by a complementor (e.g., better apps in an app store), for instance, can enhance the relevance of an incumbent platform. And even potentially disruptive innovation can play to the strengths of an incumbent firm. In other words, while some innovations are "competence destroying" for incumbents, other innovations are "competence enhancing" (Tushman and Anderson, 1986). In an example from the mid-twentieth century, the introduction of electric typewriters represented a product update that manual typewriter incumbents could potentially match while building on their existing capabilities, as Smith-Corona and Remington did in response to the success of electric models from IBM.

Competence-destroying innovation, on the other hand, opens wider capability gaps for incumbents, requiring strong dynamic capabilities to fill them. In practice, many incumbents fail to rise to the challenge due to inertia. The electronic calculator made slide rules obsolete, and digital photography has all but eliminated the once-huge emulsion film business. Even competency-enhancing challenges can overwhelm weak incumbents. The Underwood typewriter company eschewed innovation and moved too late to acquire the necessary technology to electrify, eventually being acquired by a European company that was (unsuccessfully) targeting the US market (Golder, 2000).

Complex, systemic innovations (Teece, 1984) may encompass both kinds of innovation. The innovations in electric vehicles are a combination of competence-enhancing and competence-destroying technologies with respect to auto industry incumbents. The complex internal combustion engine, with its many moving parts, is completely eliminated, but road-holding capabilities, crashworthiness, and passenger comfort technologies aren't changed nearly as much.

The cycles of change in which innovations are introduced into the market by new or existing firms and displace incumbent leaders is known as creative destruction. This goes on all the time and drives competition and productivity. It's the engine of change and progress.

Joseph Schumpeter (1942), an economist, popularized the concept of creative destruction in business and economics in the mid-twentieth century. But almost a century before him, Karl Marx had explained how capitalism was reliant on this process. *The Communist Manifesto*, for example, notes: "The bourgeoisie cannot exist without constantly revolutionising the instruments of production" (Marx and Engels, 1848/1906, p. 17).

Nevertheless, the idea was still radical when Schumpeter wrote about it. The economics discipline of his time included no provision for innovation, entrepreneurship, or technology, and it relied on models that tended toward a steady-state equilibrium. In sharp contrast, Schumpeter held that entrepreneurs and new technologies create disequilibrium, which leads to new profit opportunities. Looked at another way, Schumpeter placed innovation at the heart of economic growth. Although today innovation is often conceived of in terms of disruption and revolutionary change, Schumpeter viewed innovation as analogous to biological mutation, and creative destruction as an "evolutionary process" (Schumpeter, 1942, p. 82). The dynamic capabilities framework can guide companies as their managers choose in which area to innovate and how to best prepare the enterprise to do so, including restructuring (transformation) if. A related, capabilities-based framework in the antitrust field is called "dynamic competition" (Teece, 2023b). It is a broader concept than creative destruction because it recognizes that (nondestructive) competency-enhancing innovation can also be a driver of competition. A truly innovation-driven economy can drive waves of growth. "Innovation drives competition, and competition in turn drives innovation" (Sidak and Teece, 2009).

2.2.2 Profiting from Innovation

Managers in an innovating firm need to embed innovations in a sustainable business model that can support future innovation. This effort implicates issues of intellectual property and appropriability that can be addressed with carefully designed market entry strategies (seizing). Notably, innovators do not always profit the most from their innovation. Sometimes a fast second entrant – or even a slow third – will imitate or emulate the innovator and be able to capture most of the market. Apple's iPod was not the first standalone MP3 player, but it dominated the category for more than a decade (Cole, 2013). Merck was a pioneer in cholesterol-lowering drugs (Zocor), but Pfizer, a late entrant, secured a superior market position with Lipitor (Hilzenrath, 1998). In other cases, pioneers such as Genentech (biotechnology), Intel (microprocessors), and Dell (computer distribution) prospered for decades.

A model that helps to explain why some innovators thrive and others vanish was developed by Teece (1986, 2006, 2018c; Winter, 2006). This research has spawned a body of work that has come to be known as the profiting from innovation (PFI) model, or simply "the Teece model."[3]

Key concepts in the model are complementarities and appropriability, the extent to which the innovator can capture the profits generated by the innovation. The degree of capture is influenced by the interaction of the technology and the legal environment. Appropriability can be strong when innovations are easy to protect because knowledge about them is tacit and/or they are well protected legally. Appropriability is weak when innovations are difficult to protect, as when they can be easily imitated and/or legal protection for the relevant type of intellectual property is ineffective. For example, Laker Airways' pioneering low-price, "no frills" transatlantic service was launched to rapid success in 1977, but rivals Pan Am, TWA, and British Airways dropped their prices starting in late 1981 and the fragmented demand was insufficient to keep the thinly financed Laker in business.[4]

---

[3] See, for example, Scocco (2006); Hague (2019); and Cuofano (2023).
[4] Laker Airways owner Freddie Laker subsequently sued his rivals for conspiracy to compete by predatory pricing since they copied his pricing but not his lower cost base. He reached out-of-court settlements that helped retire his bankrupt firm's debts.

Although strategy must be set based on the appropriability regime in place at the time, appropriability regimes can change. Moreover, the regulatory regime applicable to a given innovation can be influenced by firms (Pisano and Teece, 2007). Put differently, dynamic capabilities is not only about adapting to the business environment but also about shaping it. This is one of several ways that dynamic capabilities framework goes far beyond the literature on adaptive organizations.

The essence of the PFI theory, though, is that few innovations can become profitable in isolation. Almost all innovations require the use of complementary assets and technologies (Teece, 2006), which in turn require investment. The strength of legal protection on the innovation, the ease of imitation, and the types of complements required can account for how the value generated from the innovation is distributed among the innovator, rivals, complementors, suppliers and consumers. The theory of PFI posits that profits in a business ecosystem tend to migrate to the "bottleneck" asset – that is, the asset that is needed and is hardest to replicate. This could be the innovation itself, but more often than not it also includes a complementary asset that may or may not be owned or controlled by the pioneer.

The list of critical complements includes complementary technologies and capabilities such as marketing, manufacturing, after-sale service, distribution, and software. It also includes intangible assets, such as a viable business model, customer relationships, reputations, and organizational culture. If an innovator is slow to realize the importance of complements, does not have them or cannot easily access them, it is likely to lose out to an imitator that is strong in these areas. British company EMI's CAT scanner, for example, was a sophisticated machine that required a high level of customer training, support and servicing. EMI had none of these capabilities, could not easily contract for them and was slow to realize its strategic vulnerability (Teece, 1986, p. 298). Competitors like GE with more experience selling complex healthcare equipment (along with the important complements of an experienced sales and marketing organization and a good reputation) were able to work around EMI's intellectual property and get into the market quickly with improved versions.

A corollary of the need to identify valuable complements is that non-strategic complements can usually be outsourced, provided they're supplied in the market at competitive rates. SpaceX, which has unique requirements for its pioneering vision of reusable rockets, makes most of its inputs, from rocket engines to electronics components, in-house.

Over time, though, the capabilities of the supply base can evolve. Qualcomm, for example, manufactured (through a joint venture with Sony) the mobile phones that used its proprietary CDMA chips starting in 1994 because there were no firms familiar with designing such phones. By 1999, the CDMA handset market had become sufficiently mature that Qualcomm was able to end its own manufacturing.

The points where the insource/outsource boundary should be drawn is not always clear (Chesbrough and Teece, 1996). The PFI model can help by identifying the strategic issues, but in the end it's a judgment call. Consider fabrication in the semiconductor industry. Beginning in the 1970s, AMD competed fiercely with Intel in the microprocessor market. By the 2000s, chip fabrication had become highly capital-intensive yet also increasingly available as a service. In 2008, AMD spun out its manufacturing into a joint venture with which it took a long-term supply agreement while also starting to source its processors from an established manufacturing services provider called TSMC. Intel appeared to have made the better choice and gained market share until it stumbled after 2015 while ramping up its next generation of manufacturing. Since then, it lost all of what it had gained against AMD.[5]

PFI theory provides decision criteria that are a critical part of a firm's "seizing" capability. It informs the design of the innovator's business model choice about whether to supply a complementary component or activity in-house or to contract for it (Jacobides, Knudsen, and Augier, 2006). Making this decision correctly is one of the most critical steps for securing the innovator's profitability/competitive advantage (Teece, 2010a). It requires that the innovator correctly assesses the firm's existing capabilities and/or its ability to develop new ones related to the complement in a timely, cost-effective manner.

2.2.3 Resource-Based View

Bottleneck assets, which command a profitable position, are at the heart of another theory of competitive advantage, known as the resource-based view (RBV) of the firm. It was developed in the 1980s by management scholars building on the earlier work of economists like Edith Penrose (1959) and Paul Rubin (1973). It is one of the foundations of the dynamic capabilities framework and stimulated its development, partly as a reaction to deficiencies of the RBV.

Resources are the tangible and intangible assets, broadly defined, that the firm can effectively control. These include not just physical assets, like pieces of equipment, but also abstract assets that are owned, like patents, or at least "rented," like the skills of the firm's employees.

---

[5] Intel's share of the x86 processor market grew from 72 percent in in the second quarter (Q2) of 2008 to 80 percent in Q2 2016, then fell to 64 percent in Q2 2022. The share of AMD, its only serious rival, was the mirror image, falling from 28 percent in 2008 to 20 percent in 2016, then growing to 36 percent by Q2 2022. (data from Passmark, www.cpubenchmark.net/market_share.html, accessed in August 2022).

Dynamic Capabilities: Foundational Concepts

Penrose (1959) had theorized that a firm at any point in time is likely to have underutilized resources, which creates the potential to steer their excess capacity into new lines of business to generate growth. Decades later, scholars, including Teece (1982), Rumelt (1984), and Wernerfelt (1984), picked up on the idea of resources, theorizing that a firm's control of unique resources can be a source of economies of scope and, possibly, sustainable advantage. This was further developed and popularized by Barney (1991) with the acronym VRIN because the resources most important to control are those that are *valuable, rare, inimitable,* and *nonsubstitutable*.

Yet, these cannot be the whole story behind competitive advantage, because what makes a resource valuable is how it is used. Also, what's valuable today may not be valuable tomorrow, and a good theory of competitive advantage must address these evolutionary considerations.

More fundamentally, though, it is the capability of managers to coordinate the firm's resources and channel their use into profitable activities that gives the resources their value (Spender, 1994). Others note that the term "resource" is rather vague, encompassing all manner of assets/inputs and capabilities/knowledge (Kraaijenbrink, Spender, and Groen, 2010).

Moreover, the RBV is essentially a static theory. In reality, VRIN attributes are very context-dependent, and contexts change. Resources that are rare and valuable can be undermined by new developments. Blockbuster's nationwide retail footprint became a liability when Netflix's mail-based rental system became popular. A patent may be inimitable, but it can also expire or be invented around.

A deeper issue is that the RBV offered little or no explanation or framework for deciding how a firm should develop or acquire new resources and then manage them over time. The long-term viability of a firm requires not just the amassing of key resources but also a continuous learning process, periodic pruning and augmentation, and ongoing orchestration of intangible assets and other resources. The strategic management of resources is at least as important as their mere possession. The dynamic capabilities framework accepts the VRIN criteria but is built around how VRIN resources arise in the first place and are continuously renewed. The weakness or lack of the capability to renew a firm's resources will hamper the long-run sustainability of its profits. In essence, the dynamic capabilities framework puts the resource-based view on wheels.

2.2.4 Growth-Share Matrix

A top-down approach to seizing can be found in the growth-share matrix, popularized by the Boston Consulting Group. It considers only the firm's product lines and their respective prospects. The core idea is that it is best to invest in a growing business with a healthy market share.

The growth-share matrix is a popular guide to this kind of reallocation. A matrix that crosses growth with market share was developed in the 1960s and popularized by the Boston Consulting Group through an article that appeared in a company publication (Henderson, 1970). It found increasing use during the 1970s as the conglomerate form of corporate governance became more common. The conglomerate mindset, like the growth-share matrix, views the firm as a portfolio of strategic business units to be managed like assets that can be bought and sold.

Using a 2-by-2 grid, shown in Figure 3, business units are mapped in terms of market growth and relative market share. On the vertical axis is market growth rate, and on the horizontal axis is the firm's relative market share. The four quadrants are classified as "dogs" (low growth, low share), "cash cows" (high share but low growth), "stars" (high growth, high share), or "question marks" (high growth but low share).

The matrix rests on two ideas: the "product lifecycle curve" and the "learning curve" – reasonable assumptions in many manufacturing and service businesses (Geissler and Krys, 2013). The product life-cycle curve captures the idea that products go through different stages from launch to decline, with different cash requirements at each stage. The largest cash requirements occur during a high growth phase, when firms are trying to capture the greatest market share before the industry settles down. The learning curve expresses the relationship between experience and efficiency: the more often a task is performed, the lower the cost of doing it. The implication is that the lowest cost producer will both capture a larger share and earn a larger profit per unit.

With this in mind, the quadrants of the matrix can be seen as revealing the cash flow of a business today and its prospects for the future. Businesses in the early stage of their lifecycle are likely to experience a negative net cash flow as

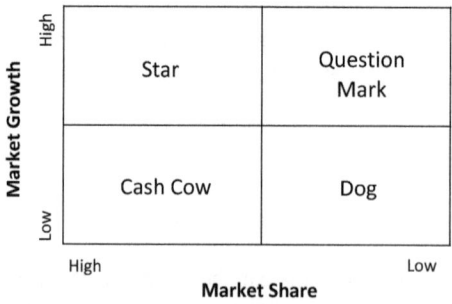

Figure 3 Growth-share matrix

the firm invests to grow and pursue market share. As a successful business matures, it should be delivering steady profits commensurate with its market share. The emphasis on cash flow is particularly relevant when the economy constrains access to capital markets, as occurred during the stagflation of the 1970s (Davis, 2016).

The most desirable type of business unit ("Star") is one experiencing high growth in which the firm has a large relative market share. It could be a maturing business in which the focal firm has helped drive rapid uptake. Businesses in this quadrant warrant significant investment to reap the benefits of continued growth. The worst ("Dog") has both low growth and low share. This may be a product line that is past its high-growth phase or that never really took off and where the focal firm has been outcompeted. The logic of the matrix is that a "dog" business should be divested or drastically rethought.

Businesses that aren't growing much but where the focal firm has a relatively large market share (assumed to translate to a cost advantage) are deemed "Cash Cows." Investment needs to be maintained but these businesses should mainly be treated as a source of cash to reinvest elsewhere. The opposite situation is a business with high growth but where the firm is a small player. This "Question Mark" could be either a growth opportunity or just a missed one. Depending on the particulars of management's intuition, internal resources, and the business climate, businesses in this quadrant may warrant further investment or they may be best divested.

The key insight is that the right time to invest heavily is in the growth phase of an industry. If significant market share fails to be won, then there's little point pouring in more funds as the industry's growth slows. This makes intuitive sense for large shifts between industries, but it may apply to frequent, smaller shifts as well.

Active reallocation of free cash flow across segments is one way to achieve the (dynamic capabilities) goal of semi-continuous transformation. A study by Lovallo et al. (2020) found an inverted-U relationship between the extent to which firms changed their investment pattern among business segments and the amount by which their return on assets exceeded the industry average. Most firms in their sample of multi-segment firms with annual sales greater than $50 million were located on the left (upward) side of the curve; that is, they would still have likely benefited from additional shifts in their allocation pattern. The same U-shaped pattern was found in a 2023 survey of more than 2,000 CEOs by professional services firm PwC; 86 percent of the firms in the survey reallocated less than 30 percent of their financial and human capital year to year and could potentially have increased their profit margins by doing more (PwC, 2024).

One problem with the matrix is that it assumes predictability, which is a risky assumption in a global economy riven by deep uncertainty. What looks like a growth industry today can stall or crash in the next period. A capabilities approach would use other criteria, supporting investment in business lines that rely on existing proprietary capabilities and sound business models. Market share is not a great metric because it reflects the past, not the future.

Corporate coherence – the relatedness of a company's capabilities – is another important dimension that the growth-share matrix fails to capture (Teece et al., 1994). Growth and market share matter, but so do the interdependencies of the firm's capabilities. Business units may interact technologically, or they may share common resources that would be too costly to maintain if one of the businesses – even a "dog" – were divested. A high-growth business that bears little relation to the firm's other activities may prove less valuable in the long run than a slightly less successful business that leverages or enhances existing capabilities. Maintaining coherence today will help growth tomorrow.

By the same token, businesses in the "Dog" quadrant could be good transformation candidates if they're a good fit. The decision to invest depends on how good management is at transforming businesses and developing fresh business models and strategies.

Companies should also invest speculatively in businesses and capabilities that are expected to be valuable in the near future and divest businesses that bear little relation to the company's capability base. The dynamic capabilities approach is generally unsympathetic to the conglomerate form of corporation, which is based on the capability-neutral notion that a good manager can manage any kind of business. True conglomerates have become increasingly rare in the major economies, although they can still be found in some industrializing nations where the market for corporate control is less well developed (Linden and Teece, 2018).

The predictable world of the growth-share matrix makes sense to the extent that it's a short-term (typically five-year) perspective on the company. The dynamic capabilities approach favors longer-term strategizing where the prospects of any given business are much less certain.

2.2.5 Simple Rules

Part of the appeal of the growth-share matrix or any similar "rule of thumb" management tool over more complex frameworks such as dynamic capabilities is that they yield straightforward rules to guide key decisions. Kathy Eisenhardt and her coauthors extended this preference to develop a theory of simple rules as a basis for strategy. As mentioned earlier, Eisenhardt had included (a limited, routine-based version of) dynamic capabilities as an example of the "simple rules" she posited as a substitute for formal strategy-making in fast-moving or uncertain markets (Eisenhardt and Martin, 2000; Eisenhardt and Sull, 2001). Simple rules, or heuristics, may cover how things are done, what things are most worth doing, when to do them, and what things not to do. An example for a large firm might be "any business line that grows larger than $1 billion must be split in two." These rules are meant to change over time, especially if they no longer seem to be working. Nor should there be too many of them. Eisenhardt and Sull (2001, p. 113) suggest a maximum of seven.

Eisenhardt and Sull (2001) contrast simple rules with two traditional views of strategy: resource accumulation (e.g., the resource-based view) and establishing and defending a position (e.g., Five Forces, which is discussed in the companion Element, *Dynamic Capabilities and Related Paradigms*). Resource and positioning strategies are one-shot models, with no guidance for sustaining competitive advantage when circumstances shift. Viewed in that way, simple rules can serve as dynamic guides for faster decisions in complex environments, avoiding analysis paralysis.

Like organizational capabilities, simple rules grow out of experience, which suggests some path dependence (and potential core rigidities). Yet Eisenhardt and Sull simply refer to firms moving fluidly from old rules to new rules when circumstances change. The managerial processes or cognition that enable this flexibility – recognizing a misalignment and identifying a solution – go unaddressed. Sull and Eisenhardt (2012) describe how rules can evolve based on analysis of the associated outcomes. But, when it comes to dropping a key rule, no insight is offered about what must surely have been a managerial decision.

Bingham and Eisenhardt (2011) filled this gap by describing a higher dynamic capability governing the addition and subtraction of the simple rules (which guide the processes they previously identified as dynamic capabilities). They call this dynamic capability simplification cycling. In one direction, firms add to the number and complexity of simple rules that they follow. In the other direction, they replace some rules and drop others entirely. In terms of the tripartite nomenclature used in this Element, simplification cycling is part of the firm's seizing activities, the means by which it pursues opportunities or other goals.

A logical implication of the addition and subtraction of rules in response to shifts in the firm's fit with the environment is that managers exercise discretion. However, Eisenhardt and colleagues seem uninterested in exploring this ability to exercise personal judgment. Instead, this stream of literature treats intuitive, entrepreneurial decision making as "improvisation" (Bingham, 2009).

Eisenhardt and her colleagues provide evidence that simple rules play an important role in organizational capabilities, particularly those mid-level capabilities I call microfoundations, such as internationalization and alliance formation (Bingham, Eisenhardt, and Furr, 2007). In the dynamic capabilities framework, however, it is the ability of top management to make idiosyncratic decisions as the situation requires that gives the firm flexibility and uniqueness (Kay, Leih, and Teece, 2018).

2.2.6 OODA Loops

An alternative approach to managing in fast-moving environments originated in the 1970s with a retired Air Force officer and instructor named Colonel John Boyd: the OODA Loop. The OODA Loop, a model of agile decision-making, has four components: Observe, Orient, Decide, and Act (Figure 4). These are often treated as purely sequential, but Boyd imagined short-loop feedback in the system as well (Rule, 2013).

"Observe" takes in signals from the external environment. "Orient" is a frame of reference or mental map of the decision space that is influenced by the decision maker's own culture, personality, and experience. "Decide" is the individual's choice based on observations conditional on orientation. "Act" then influences the external environment, leading to a new decision cycle based on the updated situation. These will unfold in real time, whether on the battlefield or in the boardroom, repeating as the situation requires. Boyd emphasized the need for continuous interaction with the external environment in order to keep mental maps updated (Watts and Augier, 2022).

There is a loose analogy between the OODA Loop and dynamic capabilities. Observation and orientation are akin to sensing and sensemaking. Deciding and acting are similar to seizing and transforming.

There are key differences as well. The OODA process, for instance, is aimed at gaining short-term wins in the course of a conflict, as opposed to longer-term competitive advantage. More importantly, the need to observe before taking action limits its applicability in situations where (unobservable) unknowns play a significant role.

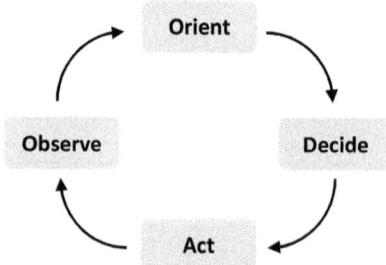

Figure 4 Diagram of an OODA Loop

Dynamic capabilities, moreover, are organizational, whereas OODA loops are conceptualized at the individual level. To implement strategy at a high level, an organization needs the agility afforded by strong dynamic capabilities as well as the tactical flexibility enabled by OODA loops. Lou Gerstner, who was a transformative CEO at IBM, observed at the start of his tenure that "you have to be fast on your feet and adaptive or else a strategy is useless" (Sellers and Kirkpatrick, 1993).

2.3 Transforming: Antecedents

A plan for seizing new opportunities often requires some degree of organizational transformation to be implemented. This could involve developing a new supply relationship, creating a new work group, or updating old routines. All changes should be regarded systemically with the goal of not unnecessarily disrupting the organization's internal alignment.

2.3.1 Transaction Costs

As we saw in the PFI model, a key question when seizing an opportunity is which activities to conduct in-house versus through outsourcing. A leading economic theory advanced to explain and guide these decisions is that firms organize their activities to minimize their transactions costs. Transaction cost theory can be traced back to a 1937 article by future Nobel laureate economist Ronald Coase (1937). Nearly forty years later this was developed into a research domain known as transaction costs economics (TCE) by another future Nobel laureate, Oliver Williamson (1975, 1985a).

A core insight in TCE is that external (contract- or market-based) activities benefit from the discipline of price, but they have an inherent weakness due to the difficulty of writing and enforcing contracts that truly cover all possible contingencies. Contractual incompleteness can sometimes allow opportunistic recontracting. Meanwhile, in-house activities offer the attractive feature of total control under all circumstances, but they are subject to the inefficiencies of bureaucratic management. Firms seek to balance the costs and benefits of each mode of governance as they choose whether a particular activity should be owned or contracted. Williamson also considered intermediate forms of organization such as strategic alliances and long-term supply relationships.

The main consideration in TCE for assessing the vulnerabilities of contract-based relationships is "asset specificity," the extent to which assets are tied to a particular relationship. When a non-redeployable investment is to be made by one party to a contract, a "fundamental transformation" occurs. Williamson (1985a) warned that large-numbers bargaining with, for example, a number of potential suppliers can collapse to one or none once any dedicated, non-redeployable investments have been made. The collapse leads to "small-numbers bargaining." In Williamson's view, because of exposure due to the inherent incompleteness of contracts, the firm that made a relationship-specific investment can become hostage to its partner, leading to the possibility of opportunistic renegotiation over the distribution of economic "rents" (profits). Because the potential risk is known in advance, the most economically efficient mode of organization for the activity would be to bring it in-house. The fear of opportunism and the migration (once transaction-specific investments are made) to strategic dependence loom large in TCE. The process whereby a competitive playing field can collapse to a small-numbers market is what Williamson called "the fundamental transformation" (Williamson, 1985a, 1985b). This occurs because transaction-specific investments reduce the set of available alternatives (e.g., suppliers) from a large number (the *ex ante* bargaining situation) to a limited choice (possibly only the one firm that made the investment).

Others have pointed out that an investment required to fulfil a contract may also deter the entry of other firms (e.g., rival suppliers), providing security that offsets the risk of becoming a hostage (Nicita and Vatiero, 2014). In practice, complex supply agreements that involve investments dedicated to a supply relationship take place all the time (De Figueiredo and Teece, 1996), as the chaos affecting global supply chains in the wake of Covid-19 lockdowns revealed.

Opportunism, as stressed by TCE, exists and ought to be – and can be – guarded against. However, the dynamic capabilities approach emphasizes building (through investment and through learning) the unique specialized resources that TCE implicitly assumes are already available for possible contracting. Dynamic capabilities also entail keeping the organization aligned with its business environment, which may require transformations such as moving activities across the in-house/contracted threshold, even though the relevant transaction costs haven't changed. It might be necessary, for example, to internalize a previously outsourced activity in order to improve the feedback across the value chain as a next-generation product is developed.

The choice of whether to position an activity inside or outside the boundary of the firm is a critical decision when seizing new opportunities. Transaction cost economics addressed a deficiency in the standard production-oriented view of the firm, which treated in-house and contracted activities interchangeably. However, as with many developments in business and economics research, it did this so narrowly that it committed the reciprocal error of holding production costs equivalent across the two options (in-house and contracted).

TCE ignores the value of integrating diverse pools of technology and know-how inside firms to facilitate knowledge sharing. A narrow focus on transaction cost issues could lead to a recommendation for outsourcing an activity that has learning and knowledge linkages to other internal operations, potentially undermining future capability development. Narrowly focused economic theories can mislead managers as well as economists.

To summarize, the TCE perspective is very narrow. It ignores processes and transformations inside the business enterprise, looking only at external supplier/alliance relationships, particularly bargaining over economic rent. While it is not a major foundational underpinning of dynamic capabilities, it has been influential and is useful in its appropriate application.

2.3.2 Evolutionary Routines

Organizational, cultural, and leadership skills are required to support organizational agility, transformation, and renewal. These skills and capabilities cannot be put into action overnight, in part because an organization tends to carry along its own legacy as it moves forward. Sometimes a radical break is worth trying if circumstances demand it. But that is as likely to create its own set of problems.

This idea that the past casts a shadow into the future is part of evolutionary economics. It is most closely associated with two heterodox economists, Richard Nelson and Sidney Winter (1982). In their model of the firm, the primary activities are building and exploiting knowledge assets, including organizational "routines." Organizational learning, in the form of processing information and solving problems, leads to new knowledge and improved routines. Because routines evolve, each firm generates a unique trajectory. Some firms are better at learning, and some firms learn the wrong lessons and eventually fail.

The routines-based approach of Nelson and Winter was an early attempt to illuminate organizational knowledge and, indirectly, organizational capabilities. However, routines, in their view, are rather static and sometimes so mired in path dependence that managers are unable to change course when necessary. This puts the routines-based approach of Nelson and Winter more in line with the organizational ecology perspective of Hannan and Freeman (1977) than with the dynamic capabilities framework. For Hannan and Freeman, change occurs in a population of firms only through "selection" among incumbents and entrants, not through firm-level adaptation or through entrepreneurial asset orchestration and the shaping of the business environment.

The dynamic capabilities framework acknowledges evolutionary thinking (and therefore recognizes some degree of path dependence), but it is a bit more optimistic and recognizes the ability of managers to be entrepreneurial and modify the design of the firm, and sometimes even its environment (Augier and Teece, 2008). With organizational learning, managers can have flashes of insight that, with board support, allow them to create new markets and transform not just their organizations but also market regulation and the attitudes of the firm's partners and customers (Denrell, Fang, and Winter, 2003; Penrose, 1959). Such transformation capabilities are a source of strategic renewal, allowing the enterprise to stay relevant (Teece, 2019a). They are a function of many factors, including governance, especially the nature of engagement by the board of directors.

In this way, the dynamic capabilities framework endeavors to integrate the evolutionary and entrepreneurial perspectives. Each brings something different. While evolutionary models sometimes allow adaptation to the environment, the dynamic capabilities approach also recognizes the ability of entrepreneurial managers to reshape their enterprise and even their business environment.

2.3.3 Organizational Behavior

The organizational design challenges that can hamper transformation capabilities are studied in the field of organizational behavior (OB). This is a major area of research that analyzes the way individuals and groups behave in an organizational setting. OB has its roots in research done in the 1920s. Management up to that time was largely focused on operational efficiency (and not innovation), as exemplified by the "scientific management" principles of Frederick Taylor (1911).

In a classic OB study, Burns and Stalker defined two ideal types of organizational structure. One was called "mechanistic," which meant clear divisions of labor, centralized authority, and steep hierarchy. The alternative was called "organic," which they used to mean an organization where individual roles are loosely defined, decision making is decentralized, and the authority structure is relatively flat. While mechanistic organizations are suitable for the pursuit of efficiency in stable markets, organic structures are better for flexibility in more dynamic environments. Put differently, organic structures support dynamic capabilities.

Some companies have successfully designed bureaucratic (mechanistic) structures for innovation (e.g., Eisenhardt and Tabrizi, 1995), but most companies have difficulty balancing bureaucracy and innovation as they grow. Even tech leader Google, according to a stream of insider complaints and other reports, is finding its innovation hampered by bureaucracy.[6] Studies (e.g., Wilden et al., 2013) have also looked at how a mechanistic structure can hinder the effectiveness of a company's dynamic capabilities more generally.

OB has three levels of analysis: the individual, work groups, and the organization (and society). Subjects include how different types of employees can be motivated, how teams can be managed effectively, how organizations can be designed, how to overcome resistance to change, and how to maintain a productive organizational culture.

In the 1930s, a number of scholars began to explore aspects of work beyond efficiency-oriented time and motion studies. Management experts such as Mary Parker Follett (1926), Elton Mayo (1933), and Chester Barnard (1938) emphasized the cooperative nature of organizations and the importance of the relations among people within them. Workers could be motivated not just through money or close supervision but also by leadership and opportunities for recognition.

There are many other topic areas within OB. One particularly important subject is how decisions are made. Economists tended to assume fully rational decision making by corporate managers. A particularly successful response to this was Nobel Prize winner Herbert Simon's concept of "bounded rationality," which recognized that decision makers are seldom able to consider a problem in all its dimensions in the perfectly optimal manner assumed in economics models (Simon, 1957). This was embraced by other scholars, such as Richard Cyert and James March, who published an influential management book about how organizational decisions are actually made (Cyert and March, 1963).

A mastery of OB issues, along with the relevant economics, is vital for building an organization with strong dynamic capabilities. OB teaches, for example, that flatter hierarchies, without layers of middle management, are generally able to make faster decisions as part of the process of seizing opportunities. And an organizational culture that embraces change, values input from all employees, and recognizes that failure is part of learning is more likely to transform readily when necessary. Meanwhile, economics teaches that incentives, governance, asset specificity, technology, and numerous other factors matter, too. When it comes to transformation, the dynamic capabilities framework is where these disparate approaches can be happily, if not neatly, joined.

All this is not to say that building dynamic capabilities in an organization and in a management team requires formal instruction. Senior executives in Silicon Valley have dynamic capabilities implicitly, almost by birthright. I'm simply identifying them explicitly in order to facilitate their more universal diffusion and extension.

---

[6] See, for example, Wakabayashi (2021); Hamel & Zanini (2022); and Amadeo (2023).

3 The Economic Theory of the Firm

In this section, I turn from the relationship of dynamic capabilities to older (but still relevant) ideas to a troubled area of academic inquiry that I sincerely hope dynamic capabilities will directly influence, namely, the theory of the firm. The economic theory of the firm grapples with questions such as (i) why firms exist in a market economy, (ii) what determines the boundaries of the firm, (iii) how firms should be organized to align incentives for managers and owners, (iv) what levels of output the firm should produce, (v) how the firm should price its products and services, and (vi) how the firm should be structured for innovation and growth. Bodies of work have grown up around these topics. But mainstream economists have neglected critical managerial issues of great economic importance such as: (i) how firms innovate (beyond just spending money on R&D), (ii) why firms have capabilities that transcend the sum of individual skills of their employees and contractors, and (iii) how some firms build and sustain competitive advantage over rivals. This third issue is the most critical yet is neglected – perhaps because economics focuses on the representative firm in perfect competition or in oligopoly. In reality, firms exhibit great heterogeneity, thereby making a mockery of most economic theories of the firm.

3.1 The Limitations of Standard Textbook Economics

The drive to establish and maintain advantages over competitors has particular economic significance because it entails implications for all the stakeholders of the firm (employees, shareholders, customers, and suppliers). In economic theory, advantage is touched on in the study of monopoly and imperfect competition, but these are structural approaches to what is fundamentally a behavioral topic.

More recently, economists have been modeling strategy-related topics such as first-mover advantage, network effects, multi-sided platforms, and switching costs, while still treating the firm as an abstraction.[7] Yet the internal drivers of these phenomena, including the development of firm-level strategy, are what ultimately matter for the success or failure of industrial policy, innovation policy, and the regulation of corporate governance. Behavioral economists have in recent years provided significant insights into decision making by businesses, consumers, and investors. But any effort to establish links between these insights and a model of the performance of individual firms has been

---

[7] Nicholas Bloom's (2017) explanation for interfirm heterogeneity as the result of knowledge-intensive firms outsourcing lower-value work, aggressively adopting IT, and benefiting from some unspecified winner-take-most mechanism is a representative example.

handicapped by the absence of a comprehensive firm-level framework such as the capabilities-based approach discussed in this Element and its companion, *Dynamic Capabilities and Related Paradigms*.

The major barrier to the acceptance of such an approach by economists is the discipline's commitment to formalism, especially mathematical models. Nobel laureate Ronald Coase, shortly before he died, contributed a column to the *Harvard Business Review*. There, Coase remarked on the field's preference for rigor over relevance: "Economics as currently presented in textbooks and taught in the classroom does not have much to do with business management", which has "severely damaged both the business community and the academic discipline . . . It is time to reengage the severely impoverished field of economics with the economy" (Coase and Wang, 2012). His plea, however, remains largely ignored by the mainstream, even as it is quietly (and, in the case of this author, not so quietly) endorsed by economists working in the fields of strategic management and evolutionary economics. The point is not that formal (dynamic) modeling isn't useful; it is. However, its tools and models need to be embedded in narratives of what happens inside real firms, industries, and ecosystems.

The problem is that mathematical formalization has too often become a key determinant of which economics studies gets published, hence how academic and even professional careers in the field advance. The incentive system driving formalization has warped the profession's perspective on how firms operate since most economists in academia know models and statistics but (unlike the author) have no experience managing actual firms.

The problem isn't new. Forty years ago, Sidney Winter and I (Teece and Winter, 1984) sketched out deficiencies and deflections in the economic treatment of firms, and little has changed. Here I will emphasize three particular concerns:

1. **Reductionism and Homogeneity:** Economists see the industry supply curve as nothing other than the sum of individual firm supply curves. This construct is convenient, especially when coupled with an assumption of firm-level homogeneity, which enables industry supply functions to be specified.[8] However, it ignores interaction effects between firms, treats them as operating on (and not above or below) an identifiable supply curve, and assumes they are producing the right product(s) given market demands. No one who encounters even a modicum of business news could

---

[8] While Alfred Marshall (1920) pioneered the concept of the representative firm as the building block for the industry supply curve, it is also the case that he used this as shorthand and acknowledged that firms are, in fact, very diverse. In *Industry and Trade* (Marshall, 1919), he was clear that firms operate in a dynamic environment and that firms themselves change. Mathematical analysis was relegated to footnotes and appendices.

possibly believe this is generally the case. The problem here is that economists took as their starting point the mathematical appendix to Alfred Marshall's (1920) *Principles of Economics* where he constructed the supply curve, rather than the body of the book and the rest of his work, which clearly recognized firm-level heterogeneity and the importance of management. In adopting this path, economists read out of the theory of the firm not only an affirmative role of the manager but also any role for entrepreneurship (Baumol, 1968, 2010). This was tragic.

2. **Neglect of Innovation and Deep Uncertainty:** Economists have preferred to focus on quantifiable risk and ignore Knightian and Rosenbergian (technological) uncertainty, despite the obvious ubiquity of deep uncertainty due to technological change, political factors, and the frequency of unforeseen events with economic implications. Uncertainty, where no specific prediction is possible, differs from risk, for which a rational decision maker (*homo economicus*, the mythical creature assumed by most economists) can apply the rules of probability. With deep uncertainty (the open set of unknown unknowns about which no forecast can be made), purely rational decision makers freeze. Keynes famously appealed to the "animal spirits" of investors and managers to drive his macroeconomic model (Keynes, 1936), but the concept didn't infuse a new theory of the firm. Economic theory needs to somehow develop a theoretical structure that allows entrepreneurs and managers to invest, learn, and decide in the presence of the deep uncertainty that is part of everyday business life. In this respect, it's worth noting that "animal spirits" (the identification of an investment path to a positive business outcome) are a manifestation of the entrepreneurial sensing activities of dynamic capabilities (Teece, 2017).

3. **Lack of Attention to Market Co-Creation:** Most economic models use firms and industries as their levels of analysis. And the firm or industry operates in a market that is assumed to exist. In reality, new markets are constantly being created by entrepreneurial acts. Market creation occurs when a manager or founder recognizes possible future sources of demand and, through determination and a leap of faith, sets out to address them (Kirzner, 1985). Market creation, especially in the digital platform era, typically takes the form of co-creation by an ecosystem, that is, a group of firms coordinated by an entrepreneur. At the outset, the future prices and preferences for a new product or service are highly uncertain. Yet the entrepreneur must build alliances with partner firms and invest in the market that they co-create. Tesla, for example, started out relying on a California company called AC Propulsion for its initial electric powertrain technology and on UK-based Lotus Cars for manufacturing and various engineering

services in order to produce its first model, the Roadster. It is an ecosystem of firms like this that initially satisfies the (previously latent) demand, if the entrepreneur's intuition proves to have been accurate, at which point rivals will inevitably start to emulate the success.

In recent decades, the economics discipline has become more serious about challenging its own assumptions. For example, behavioral economics has pointed out issues relevant to management: irrationality is possible, rule-of-thumb decision making (as opposed to optimization) is ubiquitous, and hubris and decision traps are common. These insights, while important, still leave unexplained key elements of managerially guided resource allocation such as strategy, business models, and the development of organizational capabilities.[9]

Once economists begin to accept the necessity of addressing the lacunae considered here, the theory of the firm – and microeconomics more generally – will become far more relevant and credible to other social scientists, management scholars, students, and executives. It is this very project to which I've devoted much attention in my own work because it is not enough to simply criticize. One must also build an alternative theoretical structure that affords keener insights and better explanatory power. The dynamic capabilities framework was constructed, in part, to be the foundation of a new, capability-based theory of the firm.

3.2 Existing Theories of the Firm

Economics already employs several theories of the firm. Here I briefly discuss the major variants and their shortcomings. Other approaches exist, including ownership perspectives (e.g., Hart and Moore, 1990) or the incentive perspective of Holmström and Milgrom (1994), but they are even less relevant to the true sources of firm-level distinctiveness. This section does not attempt a thorough review of the subject. Those interested can consult Hart (2011) or any number of similar reviews for a summary.

Neoclassical economics, the frame into which any theory of the firm is expected (by the mainstream) to fit, views the firm as a profit maximizing machine. The model of the firm in most economic applications could be characterized as a black box, one that mainstream economists have been reluctant to open up because inside are many phenomena not well understood. In this black-box model, the main role of management is to choose inputs so as to minimize costs while producing the level of output that equates marginal revenue with marginal cost. In other words, running the firm is modeled as a matter of simple computation that does not recognize the presence of complex

---

[9] For an account of the decades-long process of capability development at Hyundai Motor, see Teece (2025).

tradeoffs and judgments. Markets are generally assumed to exist, although demand may be uncertain. Market power (the ability of a firm to raise its prices without losing business) can exist and is almost always seen as deleterious, even if it has resulted from innovation and/or superior foresight.

One of the theories that seeks to explain why firms exist is transaction cost economics (TCE), discussed in Section 2.3.1. TCE is at best a partial theory of the firm because it implicitly assumes that production costs are the same no matter the governance arrangements (e.g., outsourcing versus vertical integration) – a highly debatable simplification. TCE offers no way to link production and governance, or to bring in innovation, which also varies with governance arrangements (Li and Tang, 2010). Coase (1937) went so far as to completely ignore revenue, a key determinant of profitability, modeling internalization of transactions up to the point where the marginal cost of internalizing an activity is equal to the marginal cost of contracting for it in the market instead. Internalization is assumed to impose costs because of bureaucratic overhead, while market contracts carry costs related to asset specificity, which introduces the risk of opportunistic recontracting. The activity being governed by either method is simply assumed to be part of a profitable business model. TCE's exclusion of production and innovation makes it not much better than neoclassical economics as a candidate for a theory of the firm.

In TCE, it is assumed that, when an asset is specific to a transaction (can't easily be productively redeployed elsewhere), then any contract across a market interface creates an opportunity for opportunistic demands by one of the parties. Another influential theory of the firm, the agency theory view, also assumes that agents will act opportunistically if allowed to do so.

Agency theory is an application of the general principal-agent model from economics, which considers the difficulty of ensuring accurate execution of intent when one entity takes actions on behalf of another, given that they may have different interests and information. Relevant principal-agent pairs include shareholders and managers, debtholders and shareholders, and managers and employees. The transmission of intent from principal to agent is seen as imposing costs, which include monitoring, bonding, and a loss that is assumed to result from the separation of ownership and management. The risk of malfeasance by managers is assumed to be all the greater because shareholders are not a uniform entity but rather composed of individuals or groups with different, possibly even competing, interests that can potentially be played off each other.[10] This concern is more or less the inverse of the capabilities view, in

---

[10] The emphasis on management opportunism obscures the hazard of shareholder opportunism driven by short-term perspectives that prefer the distribution of earnings to shareholders rather than reinvestment in the firm's production and innovation (Lazonick and Shin, 2020).

which a central role of top management is to balance the interests of various groups of shareholders, as well as balancing their interests with those of other stakeholders in the pursuit of high long-term profitability.

One of the main applications of agency theory has been to determine the optimal capital structure of the firm. In particular, Jensen and Meckling (1976) argued that the ownership structure of the corporation (insider shareholders, external shareholders, and bondholders) should be determined by considering the related agency costs. The key assumption throughout this genre of models is that managers will misuse corporate cash by undertaking negative-value projects, failing to downsize, or spending on wasteful R&D unless the cash is siphoned off to service corporate debt, dividends, or stock buybacks.

Another class of agency models pushes the problem down a level, with overspending arising from the excessive requests of division heads who are better informed than executives about the value of their projects and will choose those that yield the highest personal (as opposed to organizational) benefit (Aghion and Tirole, 1997; Rumelt, 1987). Thus, divisional managers are modeled as likely to provide inadequate or misleading information, which leads to inefficient investment (e.g., Friebel and Raith, 2010; Inderst and Klein, 2007; Stein, 2002).

The neoclassical, transactions cost, and agency theories of the firm have myriad shortcomings in terms of explaining how innovation and growth, the roots of wealth creation, are brought about. They have very little utility for management research, management education, or public policy analysis. Meanwhile, the dynamic capabilities framework makes a start at addressing the gaps and developing a theory of the firm that can assist policy and management decision makers.

Other scholars working outside mainstream economics, such as Casson (2005) and Sautet (2000), have advanced an entrepreneurial theory of the firm that also invokes capabilities and resources. Like the capabilities theory of the firm (which, in turn, invokes entrepreneurship), these are works in progress, but relatively little follow-up has occurred since their initial publications.

Somewhat more work has been done on a knowledge-based theory of the firm, beginning in the 1990s (e.g., Grant, 1996; Spender, 1996). In this approach, the firm is conceived as a "knowledge processing institution" in which the generation and application of knowledge serves as "the basis for coordination, strategic decision-making, and organizational design" (Grant and Phene, 2022, p. 5). While this makes intuitive sense, the knowledge-based view has tended to be seen as a complement to other strategic approaches to management rather than a stand-alone theory of the firm. One of its chief proponents, Robert Grant, has argued that this may be due to a split as to whether knowledge is primarily the understanding of individuals tied to objective facts or is socially constructed, deeply embedded in a specific context, and thus subjective (Grant and Phene, 2022, p. 6).

Because of the obvious affinity between the concepts of knowledge and capabilities, it is worth pondering their relationship in these regards. The dynamic capabilities framework argues that organizational capabilities are both individual and social, with the mix dependent on the type of the capability (e.g., ordinary, superordinary, dynamic) and on the maturity of the enterprise (e.g., a startup versus a large, established firm). Capabilities therefore embody the dual (personal and social) nature of knowledge.

Similar to the schism in the knowledge-based view, the capabilities approach has suffered a split between advocates of a routines-only definition and proponents (including myself) of a definition that encompasses managerial decision making as a basis of some capabilities in part or in whole. Unlike the potentially unbridgeable divide between the subjectivity and objectivity of knowledge, the difference between routines and routines-plus-management can potentially be reconciled by clearly defining the scope of the capability concept to encompass the integration of organizationally embedded capabilities with managerial cognition (Teece, 2012a). I have seen signs of progress in this regard, although the existing corpus of articles using a routines-only definition will continue to exert influence.

Another key difference with the knowledge-based view is that the dynamic capabilities framework has the support of a growing number of empirical studies verifying the relationship of capabilities to firm performance. Empirical research on the knowledge-based view remains scant. I'm therefore cautiously optimistic that a capabilities theory of the firm will eventually gain broader acceptance than the knowledge-based view.

3.3 Capabilities in Economic Theory[11]

Ideally, a capabilities theory of the firm would provide a common understanding between the management and economics disciplines. To date, most of the traffic between them has been one way, with economic models being deployed in business schools to demonstrate the seriousness of the latter.

The concept of capabilities is not completely alien to economics. Organizational capabilities have appeared periodically in the economic literature, connected most often with notions of productivity.[12] Their lineage can be traced at least to Alfred

---

[11] This section is closely based on Teece (2019b).

[12] An economic concept similar to capabilities is "organization capital." The phrase was introduced by Prescott and Visscher (1980) as a proxy for proprietary information that a firm gathers about its employees and their tasks. It has since been made more general, encompassing a firm's

Marshall, who recognized that managerial capabilities matter. Despite his use of the representative firm assumption for modelling purposes, he saw firms as being different from one another – or at least making different choices (Hague, 1958).

Penrose (1959) was one of the first economists to provide an explanation for interfirm variation, describing the relation between an individual firm's resources and its production of final products, planting the seed for the resource-based view of the firm, discussed earlier. Richardson (1972, p. 888) further developed the idea, positioning capabilities, which he defined as the firm's "knowledge, experience and skills," as the driver of, and constraint on, the activities of the firm. Demsetz (1976, p. 373) pointed to the "inherent capabilities of producers" as a possible socially benign explanation for large market shares. The term "capabilities" has continued to be used in this context (e.g., Bresnahan, 1992). More recently, Matsusaka (2001) developed a dynamic model of corporate diversification in which acquisition and divestment are driven by efforts to match a firm's activities to its capabilities. Capabilities were defined as "the combined marketing, distribution, and development skills of top and middle management" (Matsusaka, 2001, p. 428). Defined this way, they can be productively applied to additional (related) industries. Matsusaka's capabilities-based model shows why diversifications by sixty-three conglomerates from the 1960s through the 1980s would lead to positive shareholder returns. This contradicts the results of agency models, which predict that diversification will always be value-destructive.

The term "capabilities" is beginning to find its way into the economics literature, if not always using the same definition used by business scholars. John Sutton (2002) at the London School of Economics has, for the most part, equated capabilities narrowly with the ability to enhance product quality and reduce cost. In the terminology laid out earlier, such capabilities are only the "ordinary capabilities" relevant to an enterprise remaining competitive in established markets, not the dynamic capabilities that support entrepreneurial activity.[13] For Nobel laureate Amartya Sen, capabilities exist at the individual level and are the fulcrum for leveraging tangible resources into human achievement.

Capabilities or closely related concepts have even begun to appear in formal models. Although he did not use the language of capabilities, Garicano (2000) introduced a model of a knowledge-based firm in which workers are involved

---

"operating capabilities ... investment capabilities ... and innovation capabilities" (Lev and Radhakrishnan, 2005, p. 75).

[13] In an informal piece on the capabilities required for economic development, Sutton highlighted the ability (which can be classified as a dynamic capability) of managers to select promising markets (Sutton, 2012).

either in production or in solving problems. This model captures essential features of the process by which firms harness resources to develop new capabilities. This model was later embedded by Garicano and Rossi-Hansberg (2012) in a general equilibrium model in which innovations displace old products and lead to the founding of new firms. Another model that captures elements of the dynamic capabilities framework without directly referring to it was presented by Dessein and Santos (2006). In their model, firms move to one of two equilibria: a strong division of labor resulting in organizational rigidity or an internal system of flexible coordination that permits better adaptation to local changes in circumstance.

It is unfortunate, if perhaps inevitable, that the concept of capabilities finds some acceptance in modern economics primarily as a narrower notion more consistent with a static, production-function model of the firm rather than as the rich and dynamic understanding of enterprise growth in the treatments of Marshall and Penrose. This is disappointing and has deeply impaired the ability of economic theory to inform many contemporary issues. Something better is needed.

4 Building a Capabilities Theory of the Firm

The dynamic capabilities framework sketched above incorporates an entrepreneurial perspective on the firm that starts from a more primitive initial state than the one assumed in most economic models. In the Coase-Williamson transaction cost framework, for example, many markets, technologies, and prices exist already (Boudreaux and Holcombe, 1989). In reality, entrepreneurs must first cut through uncertainty and create each market before there are preferences and prices that can lead to market activity, an observation that dates back to at least the work of Frank Knight (1921). A theory of the firm incorporating elements of the dynamic capabilities framework can provide a more realistic basis for analysis.

4.1 Key Elements

A better theory of the firm would embrace many features of economic reality that are typically omitted from economic models.[14] These include pervasive deep uncertainty, the central role of non-priced assets (those not readily bought

---

[14] The capabilities framework, while antithetical to traditional production-function views of the firm, should not be seen as in strong opposition to all mainstream economic theories of the firm. The framework incorporates, but is not animated by, transaction cost or contractual concerns. While it is not blind to agency costs, these are seen as of secondary importance because the dynamic capabilities framework is focused more on opportunity than on opportunism. Managerial discretion, harnessed astutely, is seen more as a desirable complement to firm innovation and growth rather than as a significant risk factor that ought to drive organizational design and financial structure. It enables asset orchestration, which solves fundamental market failure problems.

or sold), the complexity of coordinating in the presence of complementarities, and the role of managers in orchestrating resources, which the following sections address in turn.

4.1.1 Deep Uncertainty

Deep uncertainty is ubiquitous in today's complex, interdependent business world. Major unexpected shocks, dubbed "Black Swan events" by financial theorist Nicholas Taleb (2007), occur "outside the model." Yet, as Taleb argued, such events often drive changes in the fortunes of countries and companies.

While large-scale shocks are rare, smaller shocks are fairly frequent. Small, frequent, and unanticipated shocks are particularly common in the technological arena. All industries are competing in a world where capabilities have spread to more geographic regions than ever before and interconnectedness can propagate shockwaves from once-obscure corners of the globe to major markets in the turn of a news cycle. As venture capitalist William Janeway (2012, p. 105) noted, "the Innovation Economy ... is saturated in unquantifiable uncertainty."

Nearly a century ago, Frank Knight recognized:

> With uncertainty present, doing things, the actual execution of activity, becomes in a real sense a secondary part of life; the primary problem or function is deciding what to do and how to do it. (Knight, 1921, p. 268)

Practically all of the traditional approaches to the firm implicitly assume relatively predictable environments. These approaches may recognize risk, but they ignore deep uncertainty. In effect, they assume that uncertainty can be managed in the same way as risk. Accordingly, they are of little help to managers figuring out how to compete in environments characterized by technological ferment, financial volatility, and other sources of disruption. They will misinform regulators and policy makers trying to craft regulations to control firm-level behavior and market outcomes.

Deep uncertainty is the type of operating environment then-US Secretary of Defense Donald Rumsfeld characterized in 2002 by the term "unknown unknowns."[15] A *known* unknown is when one is missing vital knowledge that could nonetheless be known, given enough time and resources. For example, in the Battle of Midway, both sides knew the enemy fleet existed, but they did not know where. In contrast, an *unknown* unknown is when we haven't even thought of the possible event.

---

[15] U.S. Department of Defense News Briefing, February 12, 2002. The phrase "unknown unknowns" was already in frequent use at NASA and perhaps appeared first in a 1982 *New Yorker* article by John Newhouse citing the example of metal fatigue causing the crash of the British de Havilland Comet airliner in the 1950s.

Uncertain events do not always result in negative outcomes. A large, unexpected event might also be positive, such as when a consumer-generated online video "goes viral" and creates massive demand for a toy or when Chinese artificial intelligence company DeepSeek launched a large language model developed at a fraction of the cost of OpenAI's ChatGPT. However, as any small company unable to take advantage of a sudden temporary surge in demand knows, positive shocks also require agile management and flexible organizations.

There is limited short-term financial protection available to guard against such uncertainty, or to embrace unexpected opportunity. Holding cash, for example, is a good hedge against positive or negative surprises, but it provides only short-term relief. Managers must still identify a path forward. Managing under deep uncertainty calls for the use of "art" as well as science. Reason and analysis are in the toolkit, but imagination is also required. In effect, navigating the unknown often involves imagining a future and endeavoring to build it.

The dynamic capabilities framework acknowledges uncertainty. That is why it prioritizes figuring out what to do when the trajectory of the business environment is uncertain and ambiguous. Many firms have proved unable to act under such conditions, which are simultaneously treacherous and full of opportunity.

When faced with deep uncertainty, doing things efficiently is of secondary importance. Yet, in companies with weak dynamic capabilities, much attention remains focused on efficiency and optimization.

To build and sustain competitive advantage, managers need to foster an organizational ability to navigate unexpected events. Many firms resort instead to crisis management, which is often all-consuming and deflects management from engaging with the full range of opportunities. What is required for sustained profitability is for the business enterprise be built to respond to the unexpected. Flexible, resilient, and opportunity-seeking (entrepreneurial) systems are a hallmark of strong dynamic capabilities.

4.1.2 Non-Priced Assets

In mainstream economics, price theory holds that with (perfect) competition it is impossible to purchase something for less than it's worth or for less than the long-term costs of producing it. If the real world looked like that, it would not support prosperity. Without the possibility of economic rents, entrepreneurial enterprises could not flourish. Yet perfect competition is precisely the condition that competition authorities allegedly seek to emulate.

In reality, and without appealing to monopoly theory, it is often possible to acquire something for less than it's worth to the buyer if the acquiring firm owns related specific complementary assets for which there is no established market.

And this is neither unusual nor unlikely. Most strategic assets have no market price in isolation because the value of an asset is context-dependent. Such assets generally yield their full value to the owner only when they are combined with other complementary or cospecialized assets. If markets for strategic assets exist at all, they are generally thin.

It is well understood that the price system's normal asset allocation role is unlikely to occur properly when asset values depend on idiosyncratic combinations without sufficient buyers and sellers to generate a market price. An economic implication of this is that input or factor markets are not fully efficient, and the factor markets will not serve their coordinating function. The entrepreneurial manager, not a Walrasian auctioneer, achieves the micro-level coordination on which the economy depends.[16] And the market inefficiency opens the way, if the entrepreneur has correctly sensed and seized opportunities, for supernormal profits derived not from arbitrage but from innovation and/or superior management acumen.

Intangibles assets are a particularly important class of strategic assets for which markets are very thin or nonexistent (Teece, 1981, 2015). This is only partially due to the limited nature of the property rights assigned to them.

Certain knowledge assets, such as context-dependent technological capabilities, cannot be meaningfully secured without acquiring a company or business unit and associated key personnel. Even if prices did reflect all information, the thin-market phenomenon (i.e., the small number of participants) would still result in wide valuation ranges (the bands in which a "competitive" price might fall) as long as firms are heterogeneous and products are differentiated. This is the setup implicitly adopted in the strategic management literature (Denrell, Fang, and Winter, 2003; Rumelt, Schendel, and Teece, 1991; Teece and Winter, 1984). Modern auction theory (e.g., Klemperer, 2002) likewise recognizes that assets will not achieve their full value in an auction if there is only one buyer.

4.1.3 Complementarity and Coordination

Technological complementarities impose coordination, market design, and control challenges. Alignment of activities within firms is required. Alignment among firms is also necessary where certain types of complementarities exist.[17]

---

[16] Léon Walras (1834–1910) pioneered the concept of general equilibrium based on a pure exchange economy in which a hypothetical auctioneer uses trial and error to find the set of prices at which all markets clear.

[17] Technological complementarities are largely absent from economic analysis. In fact, they completely vitiate the concept of a production function, which assumes that a fixed list of inputs

External alignment issues were raised decades ago at the most general level by Boulding (1956), then specifically by Malmgren (1961) and Richardson (1972). Thereafter, they were echoed by Williamson (1975), remarked upon by Teece (1984, 1990), explored empirically to a limited degree by Armour and Teece (1980) and Helfat and Teece (1987), emphasized in a vertical relation to general-purpose technologies by Bresnahan and Trajtenberg (1995) and Helpman (1998), but never fully explored or developed by economists or management scholars. The economics literature tends to assume that, in the main, upstream and downstream investment expectations will converge, which seems unlikely given the proprietary (and hence at least partially secret) nature of much of knowledge required for investment activity.[18]

In the economically significant realm of enabling and general-purpose technologies, these alignment problems are particularly severe. Bresnahan and Helpman are among the few pointing out potential contractual and market failure issues that may lead to underinvestment. With reference to this class of widely applicable technologies, Jones (2012, p. 660) noted that the main problem for capturing value by exploiting the application of an innovation in many downstream sectors is "the fact that you cannot identify the recombinant possibilities ex ante means that you cannot easily solve the bargaining problem in practice – you cannot integrate your way around it. So innovation faces a serious market failure in the sense that socially profitable innovation does not occur."

In short, the market, and perhaps even vertical (and horizontal) integration, cannot ensure socially optimal innovation and adoption of general-purpose and enabling technologies.

From a managerial perspective, there is a similar lacuna regarding "alignment." Some of these concerns are addressed under the heading of business model issues (Teece, 2010a), leaving it to entrepreneurs to design creative organizational arrangements to help solve the coordination and associated appropriability challenges. When the coordination/integration challenges are external, private ordering (contractual) solutions are possible in some – but not all – cases.

---

is used to practice a technology known to all firms. In reality, production functions, even in the absence of a major innovation, are often firm-specific and quite proprietary. While Schumpeter (1934) equated innovation with "new combinations," his theory brought no granularity to the analysis. Nor did he consider the appropriability issues around new combinations of assets with different owners because his main focus was on the ability of new products and processes to displace existing ones. This spoke to substitution, not complementarities.

[18] Vertical integration can partially mitigate coordination problems. Armour and Teece (1980) established that R&D levels in the petroleum industry were sensitive to the extent of vertical integration in a direction suggesting that integration can ease the coordination issues when new technology is developed and deployed. Helfat and Teece (1987) showed that vertical integration reduced risk, which can include the uncertainty that accompanies commercialization of new technology.

Economic theory has yet to address these pervasive market imperfections in a meaningful way, particularly as regards their implications for the theory of the firm, the role of the manager, and the challenges associated with innovation. Hints about these matters can be found in Richardson (1972) and in the literature on entrepreneurship (e.g., Kirzner, 1997) and that on general-purpose technological innovation (Bresnahan and Trajtenberg, 1995; Helpman, 1998; Jones, 2012). What is missing is an effort to tie these disparate threads into a theory of the firm that includes the decisive role of managers. The dynamic capabilities framework can move the theory of the firm in that direction (Teece, 2010b, 2017).

4.1.4 Managerial Asset Orchestration

Special value can accrue to the enterprise that achieves good internal and external asset alignment. Because many asset markets are thin, the value-enhancing coordination and alignment of assets/resources is difficult to achieve through the price system and is more easily accomplished by managerial fiat (i.e., with direct ownership of the assets). Achieving alignment through such internalization goes beyond what Barnard (1938) has suggested as the functions of the executive. His was a limited view of managers, with their task whittled down, in the words of Williamson (1993), to one of "cooperative adaptation." Building and assembling assets inside the firm (as opposed to accessing them through a skein of contracts) is not done primarily to guard against opportunism and recontracting hazards, although in some cases that may be important. Rather, it is done to achieve economies of scope and appropriability benefits, which goes far beyond the conventional economic logic of minimizing Williamsonian transaction costs. This alignment process has incentive and organizational culture dimensions, too. It is meaningful that the basic unit of analysis for dynamic capabilities is not the transaction (as in transaction cost economics) but the entire firm (see Section 4.3.2).[19]

In a capabilities-based theory of the firm, the concept of cospecialization between or among assets is particularly important (Teece, 1986). Assets that are cospecialized need to be employed in conjunction with each other, usually inside the firm (Teece, 1980).

Merely putting two business units or departments under common ownership and common governance need not bring about "integration" in the sense of achieving full alignment and cooperation. That requires wise managerial oversight and active coordination efforts to overcome the bureaucratic

---

[19] The dynamic capabilities framework is sensitive to issues around contracts (explicit or implicit). However, unlike TCE, it places considerable emphasis on production, learning, and innovation.

disadvantages of integration. The disadvantages Williamson identified include communication distortions, internal procurement hazards, internal expansion proclivities, and program persistence because "shifting the incremental transaction from the market to the firm generally results in greater budget-based supports, whence vertical integration gives rise to persistence tendencies" (Williamson, 1975, p. 122). His concluding comment was that

> although market failure constitutes a presumptive basis for internalizing transactions, the "defects" associated with market exchange may need to exceed a nontrivial threshold before internal organization offers a clear cost advantage. (Williamson, 1975, p. 130)

Some degree of integration capability (whether within a firm or among firms) is necessary for long-term survival. Successful functional integration can be tremendously hard, especially in contrast with disaggregation, which is often simple to accomplish. Growth will always involve more work on integration (which may be one reason why many managers settle for low growth). The entrepreneurial task of implementing value-enhancing "new combinations" inherently requires some measure of functional integration. The same is true for new business models and the introduction of new capabilities.

The challenge of functional integration is less formidable in smaller companies. The CEO/founder can use personal influence to help bring it about. As organizations become larger, the CEO must work through others to communicate goals, motivate employees, and propagate the organizational culture that underpins good alignment. As entrepreneur Peter Thiel has noted, this is hard to do, but he credits his fellow PayPal co-founder, Elon Musk, with these capabilities. With reference to Musk's Tesla and SpaceX ventures, Thiel has said that "what was really impressive was integrating all these pieces together," and that this "is actually done surprisingly little today and . . . when people can pull it off, is very valuable" (Thiel, 2014).

In the dynamic capabilities framework, rather than the single-minded pursuit of cost minimization, the distinctive role of the (entrepreneurial) manager is this "orchestration" of cospecialized assets and of business activities to achieve value-creating and value-capturing alignment. Performed astutely and proactively, such orchestration can: (1) keep cospecialized assets (and people) in value-creating alignment, (2) identify new cospecialized assets to be developed through investment, and (3) divest or run down cospecialized assets that no longer yield special value. These goals contribute to organizational prosperity and could not be readily achieved by accessing a similar set of assets through a web of contracts with external partners in part because of dynamic transaction costs (the costs of negotiating and so on) but also because there may not be a competent entity to build or supply the assets that are needed. And even if there were, accessing the assets via contracts would likely lead to what Williamson (1975, 1985a) called a small numbers bargaining problem, which would undermine value capture. In other words, highly specialized capabilities must often be built because they cannot be bought (and there is limited utility in labelling this a transaction cost problem). Judging the best approach for accessing and coordinating necessary assets and effectuating their effective orchestration are critical functions of managers in the dynamic capabilities framework.

4.2 Toward a Capability-Based Theory of Heterogeneous Firms

As mentioned earlier, economic theory has difficulty explaining the distinctiveness of firms and why certain firms excel. This interfirm heterogeneity stands in opposition to the common economic simplification of interchangeable firms or of firms with characteristics drawn from a known distribution.

Robert Gibbons (2005) grouped theories of the firm into four clusters, one of which relates to resources, routines, and knowledge. These are the essential components of organizational capabilities, and he saw "mouth-watering potential implications" of this cluster for a future formal theory of the firm (Gibbons, 2005, p. 202). Formalization of these concepts is, however, extremely difficult, and attempts to model them are doomed either to fail or to simplify them into a useless abstraction. Great progress, however, can be made building what Nelson and Winter (1982) called "appreciative theory," meaning one that is qualitative but rooted in real-world observations.

This section is a contribution toward using a capabilities perspective to develop a more realistic, less caricatured, theory of the firm. The sketch that follows is informal, but that need not be a bar to theory development. There have been such cases in other fields. The theory of plate tectonics, for example, has its origins in the work of Alfred Wegener, a German meteorologist. Starting in 1912, he advocated a theory of continental drift, assembling evidence that supported a hypothesis that Eurasia and the Americas had once been joined, but without identifying a formal mechanism by which their separation could have occurred. Controversial in Wegener's time, the theory is now scientific conventional wisdom as part of the formal theory of plate tectonics, which developed over decades.

As the philosopher Bertrand Russell wrote of theory development, "Beginnings are apt to be crude, but their originality should not be overlooked on this account" (Russell, 1946/1972, p. 126–127). The following account of a nascent theory may eventually be regarded as crude after further development has taken place. That would be preferable to it being overlooked by those it could assist.

4.2.1 Introduction

As discussed in Section 3, economic models typically use a "representative firm" abstraction to explore market structures of perfect competition and oligopoly. While it has long been recognized that most industries contain "strategic groups" of firms pursuing similar business models (Porter, 1979) for which a representative firm assumption might be benign, that assumption can shed no light on the considerable heterogeneity among firms across an entire industry. A theory that cannot account for the differences among, for example, Tesla, Mercedes-Benz, General Motors, Honda, and Hyundai is of limited utility for explaining behaviors and outcomes in the automotive industry.

This heterogeneity has roots in both demand- and supply-side factors. Differences among firms often reflect the fact that firms target different customer segments with different needs. Thus, in autos, Volkswagen competes for different customers than Rolls-Royce, and this requires different production technologies and different marketing and sales methods. Even when firms are pursuing the same or similar market segments, they may opt for different technological and organizational approaches, use different business models, and choose different strategies for any number of reasons. Such (strategic) decisions by managers establish different pathways, leading to interfirm heterogeneity.

Deep uncertainty also drives interfirm differences. Technological uncertainty renders decisions relating to innovation complex, and different firms make different decisions because of how each management team reads the situation (Rosenberg, 1982; Teece, Peteraf, and Leih, 2016).

The dynamic capabilities framework thus recognizes the distinctive role of managers in asset orchestration and recombination. In endeavoring to build a theory of the firm without fully acknowledging the economic importance of internally managed coordination, Williamson, Jensen, and others have deflected attention away from the important role that the business enterprise, led by entrepreneurs and managers, plays in allocating resources as it expands the economy's existing set of possibilities.

By contrast, neoclassical economics treats managers as little more than a set of algorithms. To determine production levels, they use the point where marginal revenue equals marginal cost. They set wages equal to the marginal revenue product of labor. They optimize capital structure using the relative prices and tax treatment of equity and debt. The contrast of these rules with the vital roles that managers play in real firms (and in the dynamic capabilities framework) couldn't be more stark.

4.2.2 Sensing, Seizing, and Transforming

The sensing, seizing, and transforming capabilities of managers and their organizations bring learning and leadership into the theory of the firm. Most importantly, they are the critical factors that distinguish between what can be done inside the firm as opposed to what is possible under a system of pure contracts.

"Sensing" is an inherently entrepreneurial set of activities that involves exploring technological opportunities, probing markets, and listening to customers, along with scanning the other elements of the business ecosystem. It requires management to build and test hypotheses about market and technological evolution, including the recognition of latent demand. The world wasn't clamoring for a coffee house on every corner, but Starbucks, under the guidance of Howard Schultz, recognized and then successfully developed and exploited the potential new market. As this example implies, sensing requires managerial insight and vision – or an analytical process embedded in the enterprise that can serve as a proxy for it. Sensing benefits from the application of data analytics and artificial intelligence to real-time market data to spot trends, anomalies and patterns. The ability to sense different ways of doing things is the precursor to choosing among them.

Once opportunities are sensed, choices must be made, and investment follows. The structure and assets of the organization help shape the choices made. "Seizing" includes designing and implementing a business model to satisfy customers, shape markets, and capture value. Large cash balances, or ready access to external capital, provide financial flexibility that aids dynamic capabilities. Top talent helps. Employee motivation and cultural alignment are vital. Good incentive design is a necessary but not sufficient condition for superior performance in this regard; good leadership is critical. Strong external relationships must also be forged with suppliers, complementors and customers, with the boundaries of the firm drawn to avoid (or at least limit) the loss of profits to the owner of an external "bottleneck" asset (Teece, 1986).

Sensing and seizing are similar to exploration and exploitation, two activities discussed in the organizational behavior literature as potentially incompatible inside a single organization (March, 1991). Exploration (e.g., research on a potentially disruptive technology) has a longer time horizon and greater uncertainty than exploitation (e.g., selling mature products). The two types of activities require different management styles. One solution is an "ambidextrous organization" where two separate subunits with different cultures are linked by shared company-wide values and senior managers with a broad view (O'Reilly and Tushman, 2004, 2013). But the tensions between subunits must still be astutely managed so that the integrated structure reaps the full learning benefits.

A firm's "Transforming" capabilities draw on management's leadership skills in order to avoid undermining employee morale. The need for a realignment of the enterprise's resources is most apparent when radical new opportunities are to be addressed. But more modest changes are needed periodically to soften the rigidities that develop over time from asset accumulation, standard operating procedures and insider misappropriation of rent streams. A firm must also maintain strategic alignment vis-à-vis its ecosystem. Complementarities need to be constantly managed and reconfigured as necessary to achieve evolutionary fitness, limiting loss of value in the event that demand shifts in a way that favors external complements.

Existing theories account for a firm's configuration at a point in time, possibly allowing for its response to a one-time change such as a shift in transaction costs. Few economists, though, have attempted to build a theory of the durable growth of the firm. The incorporation of dynamic capabilities (sensing, seizing, and transforming) in a theory of the firm as a set of ongoing activities opens avenues for the firm to evolve in response to any number of shocks and to compete on the basis of innovation, not just cost minimization.

4.2.3 The (Normative) Economics of Organizational Agility[20]

The dynamic capabilities framework indicates a set of principles that entrepreneurial managers should and usually do understand. In particular, managers must recognize that the pursuit of agility (which entails speed, flexibility, and resilience) often puts ordinary and dynamic capabilities in conflict. Observers note that "in attempting to preserve their source of advantage, organizations can overcommit to institutionalization, making them more inert and vulnerable to environmental shifts" (Worley, Williams, and Lawler, 2014). Achieving organizational agility, however, can require sacrificing technical efficiencies in favor of assets and structures that can be more easily redeployed when necessary. The net benefits (that is, benefits minus costs) of organizational agility increase with the degree of uncertainty in the organization's competitive environment.[21] Strong dynamic capabilities can yield organizational agility while minimizing the cost of achieving it.

The trade-off between agility and efficiency is only sometimes recognized in the field of economics (e.g., Stigler, 1939). It has likewise received insufficient attention in the field of strategic management and is almost never mentioned in

---

[20] This section is based on Teece, Peteraf, and Leih (2016).
[21] The concept of high-velocity markets is similar (Bourgeois and Eisenhardt, 1988).

Dynamic Capabilities: Foundational Concepts

organizational theory. The closest parallel is the trade-off between efficiency and innovation addressed in the organizational ambidexterity literature by Michael Tushman, Charles O'Reilly, and colleagues (e.g., Benner and Tushman, 2003; Tushman and O'Reilly, 1996). Only very limited attempts have so far been made to offer prescriptive advice to managers regarding how to negotiate the agility-efficiency trade-off.

An important issue is what level of agility is worth pursuing, given that maintaining agility comes with ongoing costs (see, e.g., Ifandoudas and Chapman, 2009). Not all business environments involve deep uncertainty at all times. A relatively calm environment allows for "business as usual" to carry on indefinitely. Every organization, though, wants to be ready for agile change when needed, which should inform choices such as asset purchases and organizational design. Manufacturers, for example, can invest in more flexible types of plants and equipment that can deal with frequent changes in the rate of production and be fully or partially redeployed as requirements shift. In other cases, agility will be sacrificed to aid strategy, as in the case of commitments to production capacity.

An excellent example of the interdependence of agility (a capability) and strategy taken from the military context is the Battle of Trafalgar (off Cape Trafalgar, Spain) in 1805. This was a naval engagement fought by the British Royal Navy against the combined French and Spanish fleets during the Napoleonic Wars. Historians never fail to give credit to the British Admiral Lord Nelson's strategy: engaging the enemy fleet by dividing his smaller force into two columns directed perpendicular to the larger enemy fleet – a complete break from prevailing tactical orthodoxy (which was to engage parallel, in a single line). Less frequently mentioned is that in pursuing this strategy, Admiral Nelson hoped to isolate the enemy's flagship (leading to a lack of coordination) and create chaos on the water. In the ensuing chaos, there would necessarily be ship-to-ship actions, in which Admiral Nelson's more agile ships and crews would have a better chance. Lord Nelson knew that the better seamanship and faster reloading speeds of the Royal Navy gunners would play a key role. The strategy would favor his ships' and his crew's capabilities over their Spanish and French adversaries. In short, Admiral Nelson's strategy leveraged the more agile capability of his naval force. Despite a smaller number of ships, he was able to pull off a decisive victory.

Lord Nelson's victory at Trafalgar was not through strategy alone, as is often assumed, but from the marriage of strategy with capabilities (and, in particular, agility). Agility can be costly and will not yield commensurate benefits unless married to a good strategy.

As this example suggests, the level and type of agility that (entrepreneurial) managers choose to build into their organizations and maintain should depend not just on the uncertainty in the business environment but also on their strategy, on the firm's positioning in the market, and on the weighting assigned to downside and upside risks. That said, firms with strong dynamic capabilities will be better at sensing emerging developments, helping them to achieve agility with less sacrifice of efficiency.

The dynamic capabilities framework, which encompasses strategy, helps to understand when to build agility in, when not to, and when to sacrifice it. The framework highlights interrelationships that help set priorities and enable coherence and congruence between strategy, structure, and the business environment.[22] This is a complex balancing process with no single "best" arrangement. Hence, each firm, based on its management, its legacy elements, and its current circumstances, will solve the challenge in a distinctive fashion.

4.2.4 The Foundations of Firm-Level Heterogeneity

With the dynamic capabilities framework, I believe that we are a few steps closer to a truly fundamental understanding of the origins of firm-level heterogeneity and the sources of enterprise-level value creation, value capture, and value distribution, along with durable growth. No other framework is as ambitious in its reach.

Uncovering the origins of long-term cash flow generation is the deepest inquiry in microeconomic and financial theory. It is the concern that directly and indirectly animates management theory and investment choices and motivates the quest for understanding the ways that actual enterprises are far from their too-frequent representation as interchangeable black boxes.

A top management team determines the path and character of an organization. At any given date, the top management team of a particular enterprise is unique to it alone. While the organization and its capabilities provide managers with the raw material required to perpetuate the enterprise, it is incumbent on top management to make the key decisions as to whether the enterprise is currently making the right products and addressing the right market segment and whether its future plans are appropriately matched to consumer needs and technological and competitive opportunities. Top management must develop conjectures, validate them, and realign assets and competences for new requirements, as well as shaping the internal culture in which the generation and sharing of knowledge take place. The combined dynamic capabilities of the managers and the organization enable the enterprise to profitably orchestrate its

---

[22] In this regard, the framework endeavors to revitalize the application of general systems theory in management. One needs, as Boulding noted, to "not seek . . . to establish a single, self-contained 'general theory of practically everything' . . . Such a theory would be almost without content, for we always pay for generality by sacrificing content, and all we can say about practically everything is almost nothing" (Boulding, 1956, p. 197). The dynamic capabilities framework endeavors to balance attention between the forest and the trees.

Dynamic Capabilities: Foundational Concepts

resources, competences, and other assets particularly those that are co-specialized (Pitelis and Teece, 2009).

The business processes at the heart of capabilities can be unique and firm-specific. These unique processes are sometimes called "signature processes" (Gratton and Ghoshal, 2005). I introduced them earlier in the context of super-ordinary capabilities, but such processes can also be part of the firm's dynamic capabilities. They develop from the firm's past activities, irreversible investments, and embedded values, which constitute a distinct organizational heritage. They are also influenced by the needs of the particular customer segments that a business enterprise chooses to target.

The basis of signature processes in past managerial decisions tends to make them difficult for competitors to imitate. Sooner or later, though, if they are good, they will be copied. The Toyota System of Production, which was eventually matched by US and European automotive firms, is one such example. However, the replicability of any complex process is sometimes confounded by what Lippman and Rumelt (1982) call "uncertain imitability" because even the people involved may not fully understand the complementarities underlying a specific capability. This, along with a high tacit component to the underlying knowledge, may keep a signature process effectively proprietary for quite some time, providing at least a temporary source of interfirm heterogeneity.

4.3 Contrast with the Transaction Cost Theory of the Firm

In some ways, but not in others, the dynamic capabilities approach is consistent with the Coase-Williamson transaction costs perspective described in Section 3.3.1. Both frameworks recognize that the firm and markets are alternative governance options. Here, though, I want to compare what dynamic capabilities and transaction costs bring to a theory of the firm, particularly how they account for the boundaries of the firm, which is considered to be one of the strengths of the transaction cost approach.

4.3.1 Nontradable Assets

For Williamson, the determination of what belongs inside and outside the firm is based on transaction costs, including the costs and risks of writing contracts with buyers, suppliers, and alliance partners. In the dynamic capabilities framework, the selection of what to organize internally versus via alliances or the market depends on the availability and the nontradability of assets, on capabilities, and to some extent on what Langlois has termed "dynamic transaction costs," namely, "the costs of persuading, negotiating, coordinating and teaching outside suppliers" (Langlois, 1992, p. 113).

The notion of nontradability (related to the issue of non-priced assets in Section 4.1.2) does not precisely match Williamson's concept of transaction costs because there are reasons beyond the asset specificity analyzed by Williamson that assets, particularly intangibles, will be nontraded or thinly traded. For example, there may simply be no viable business model for licensing certain types of know-how, or certain assets may be so idiosyncratic that they aren't productive anywhere else.

Moreover, many companies will simply not license "strategic" technological assets, such as Coca-Cola's secret formula for its namesake beverage concentrate, at any price. One reason might be that both parties are able to sell in the same territory and territorial restrictions are not allowed in a contract (possibly for antitrust reasons) or are not enforceable at low cost. Theoretically, a licensor ought to be indifferent between own sales and the sales of a licensee if the royalty rate is set to enable royalties to equal lost profits. However, such arrangements are rarely, if ever, seen, in part because there is likely to be ambiguity with respect to which customers and what sales are actually lost to the licensee. There are also likely concerns about the licensee rather than the licensor capturing the "learning by using" know-how associated with exploiting the technology. More generally, technology licensing may not be feasible due to differences in expectations with respect to the technology's profit potential. This may open such a wide bargaining range that the positions never converge and no transaction can occur.

As Williamson's framework suggests, negotiating, contractually specifying, and monitoring any sharing arrangements are also likely to be very difficult. However, such contract-related transaction costs do not address the competitive and knowledge-related challenges associated with the licensing of strategic technologies described in the preceding paragraph. Thus, it is rare that firms will be able to rely entirely on an unbundled business model in which the licensing of patents or trade secrets can be used as a mechanism to capture value from know-how. Rambus, Inc, and Dolby Labs are amongst the exceptions, and both these companies have had challenges.

4.3.2 Level of Analysis

Another distinction between dynamic capabilities and transaction costs is the level of analysis. The basic unit of analysis for dynamic capabilities is not the transaction (as in transactions cost economics) but the firm (and its business environment). This orientation allows a capabilities-based analysis of internal and external alignments, which is a necessary condition for correctly analyzing the value-enhancing potential of cospecialized assets. A firm-level perspective allows an emphasis on production, learning, and innovation, while transaction cost economics is limited to the analysis of contracts and risks. The dynamic capabilities framework is less concerned with avoiding opportunism and more concerned with embracing opportunity.

This difference in level of analysis can be seen in terms of how the boundaries of the firm are analyzed. The question is usually framed in terms of vertical supply relationships: should a particular activity be conducted in-house or outsourced? But at the level of the firm, the question is also one of horizontal scope: in what product markets should a firm compete?

Teece et al. (1994) provided a capabilities-aware framework that endeavored to account for the horizontal boundaries of the firm based on learning, path dependencies, technological opportunities, the selection environment, and the firm's position in complementary assets. Management's ongoing reassessments of the firm's coherence in product space are part of its dynamic capabilities.

4.3.3 Cospecialized Assets

As discussed in Section 4.1.4, Williamson recognized that cospecialized assets may require a single owner, but he retained a bias for market-based contracting below some undefined threshold. In prior research on technology management and the boundaries of the firm, Teece (1980, 1982, 1986) saw cospecialized assets as important building blocks to explain differences in firms' technology strategies and capabilities.

Building and assembling cospecialized assets inside the firm (rather than accessing them through a skein of contracts) is not done primarily to guard against opportunism and recontracting. Instead, because effective coordination and alignment of assets is difficult to achieve through the price system, good alignment is better accomplished inside the firm. Performed astutely and proactively, the orchestration of cospecialized assets by entrepreneurial managers can: (1) keep cospecialized assets in value-creating and value-capturing alignment; (2) help identify new cospecialized assets to be developed through investment; and (3) support the divestment or running down of cospecialized assets that no longer yield special value. These goals cannot be readily achieved through contractual mechanisms in part because of dynamic transaction costs (the costs of negotiating, etc.) but also because there may not be a competent entity to build or "supply" the assets that are needed in the first place (i.e., the markets are too thin or simply nonexistent). In other words, capabilities must often be built, they cannot be bought, and there is limited utility in labeling this conundrum as a transactions cost problem.

Rather than stressing opportunism (while noting that opportunism must still be guarded against), the emphasis in dynamic capabilities is on investing and, in particular, building specialized assets (that often cannot be bought) and on effectuating changes needed to keep the enterprise aligned with its business environment. Such changes include research and development, redesigning the business model, and asset selection.

4.3.4 The Coordination of Systemic Innovation

A related consideration is the choice of whether to rely on external suppliers for complementary innovations. This is related to what Richardson (1960) and Williamson (1975) have called "convergence of expectations." Complementary innovations require investments in research and development to be coordinated, which can be difficult to effectuate using contractual mechanisms.

Coordination is of greatest concern when innovation is systemic (Teece, 1984). Systemic innovation involves elements of a system for which the designs must be harmonized due to their technological interdependence. The interdependence can be intrinsic. An airplane, for instance, is a complex assembly of parts and subsystems with extremely tight tolerances. If not designed holistically, problems are likely to emerge late in the process and require considerable resources to identify and fix. In other cases, interdependence can result from the choice of a business model. In smartphones, Apple chose to keep its operating system and hardware intimately linked, while Google concentrated on software that it could license to multiple phone manufacturers. As the Apple example suggests, a systemic design process need not be a barrier to the outsourcing of production.

Autonomous innovations, which do not require coordinated activities between parties, can occur quite easily inside separate organizations then be "plugged in" to the bigger project thanks to public or private interface standards. For example, the open architecture of the IBM personal computer allowed competitive innovation to thrive for many of its subsystems, including hard drives and monitors.

In some cases of systemic innovation, the involvement of one or more specialized partners in the design process is unavoidable. The lenses in semiconductor manufacturing equipment come from specialists such as Germany's Zeiss, which must co-design a subsystem with an equipment maker such as ASML of the Netherlands for use in ASML's microchip lithography tools. The collaboration of multiple enterprises in a systemic innovation introduces many hazards that do not comfortably fit within the rubric of transaction costs. Delays are common and may result from miscommunication, limited capabilities, and divergent goals amongst the parties.

Harmonization of development among firms is particularly difficult when capabilities are very unequal. Boeing discovered this to its cost when it decided to rely on a global array of suppliers to develop parts for its new 787 Dreamliner as a cost-sharing measure; some suppliers lacked the capabilities to develop

Dynamic Capabilities: Foundational Concepts

parts of the necessary quality, and Boeing had cut back its monitoring capability. Deficits in the capabilities of suppliers resulted in years of delay (Michaels and Sanders, 2009). It is not entirely clear, from the perspective of theory, whether this is best viewed as a contracting problem or a capabilities issue. However, the latter appears to be more powerful.

The Boeing experience echoes Lockheed's experience three decades earlier when the L1011 wide bodied plane was delayed by the failure of Rolls Royce to develop and deliver on time the RB211 jet engine for the L1011, effectively putting Lockheed out of the wide-bodied civilian aircraft industry. This was not an exercise of opportunism by Rolls Royce; rather it reflected Rolls Royce's lack of ability to achieve ambitious technological goals.

In the presence of these hazards, maintaining technological control of the innovation trajectory sometimes requires vertical integration (and heavy investment in R&D). When this is not possible, the dynamic capabilities framework points to (re)shaping the industry's architecture through measures such as corporate venture investments in the supply base to build a competitive market for key complements (Pisano and Teece, 2007).

4.3.5 The Coordination of Knowledge Workers

Inside the enterprise, transaction cost economics and other contractual perspectives on the firm see employees as more or less interchangeable. A tradition dating back to Alchian and Demsetz (1972) emphasizes that teamwork, monitoring and coordination are facilitated by occurring inside a firm, where shirking can more easily be monitored. This branch of the theory of the firm tends to focus on incentive design and verification.

However, this approach ignores how the firm's expert talent – the knowledge workers providing the creative solutions to the firm's challenges – must be managed (Teece, 2011b). Managing expert talent has less to do with metering and monitoring to detect and punish shirking and other forms of opportunism than it has to do with detecting, monitoring, and calibrating potentialities.

Alchian, Demsetz, and Williamson have all emphasized opportunistic free riding as the key hazard to guard against. Williamson assumes, correctly, that human actors are boundedly rational and self-interested.

By contrast, the dynamic capabilities framework emphasizes other traits of human nature, namely (1) entrepreneurship and willingness (when properly incented) to pursue high-risk/high-reward opportunities, and (2) foresight and acumen. These are undoubtedly less ubiquitous and evenly distributed than self-interest, but they are far more salient for value creation and must be recognized and cultivated by managers using a light touch.

In the dynamic capabilities framework, opportunism is not held in abeyance, nor are incentive issues ignored. But these are usually of secondary importance. The long-term viability of the firm is of prime importance, and it lies in the generation, configuration, and leveraging of knowledge assets, including human capital.

4.3.6 Beyond the Boundaries of the Firm

While the analysis of the boundaries of the firm captures many key elements of managing value creation, the fundamental problems to be solved by the firm are the design and implementation of value capture strategies in an uncertain environment. These strategies must overcome any appropriability problems and help create the new organizational capabilities needed to address fresh opportunities. While this is plainly in the realm of strategic management and dynamic capabilities, it is also basic to the nature of the firm.

The advantages of organizing economic activity inside the firm go well beyond savings in transaction costs. In particular, the advantages flow from the ability of entrepreneurial managers to combine idiosyncratic assets that are cospecialized and often nontradable to create and capture value by offering distinctive services (solutions) to customers while ensuring a return on investment adequate to fund ongoing activities. To a first approximation, the concerns of transaction cost economics are unnecessary baggage. For instance, if one wants to understand issues surrounding creating value, not simply protecting value created, transaction costs are at most a fraction of the story. The firm's routines for sensing, seizing, and transforming can provide a basis for profitability well beyond the efficient minimization of contracting costs and hazards.

Opportunism is controlled not just through metrics and monitoring, but also through high commitment cultures. A transaction-level theory cannot encompass such enterprise-scale phenomena. Innovative firms typically need strong values because it's hard in the loosely structured internal environments that innovation requires to define and measure performance and implement rigid controls. Creative and entrepreneurial activity need to be rewarded as well as encouraged. But creative talent thrives in a high-trust environment with challenging objectives.

The dynamic capabilities framework suggests a new theory of the firm, that is nonetheless consistent with the observation of the pioneering Cambridge University economist Alfred Marshall (1898, p.213) that "capital consists in a great part in knowledge and organization: and of this some part is private property and the other part is not. Knowledge is our most powerful engine of production—organization aids knowledge." Sadly, Marshall's deep understanding of the firm fell by the wayside as his modeling exercises inspired modern economics. The capabilities-based theory of the firm proposed here opens up the black box of the firm and challenges economic theory to analyze new dimensions of innovative and productive activity, including value capture as well as value creation.

Put differently, the dynamic capabilities framework paves the way for a "doing" theory of the firm. Mainstream economic theories of the firm are about the firm "being." The static assumption of equilibrium in the traditional theory prevents any exploration of how the firm innovates and achieves profitability. Moreover, disequilibrium is the true state of markets as they experience successive waves of creative destruction. Understanding the processes and activities which enable firms to survive and prosper under uncertainty and disequilibrium are just as important if not more so than understanding why they exist or the boundaries and structures they have chosen. A dynamic orientation is critical.

5 Conclusions

The dynamic capabilities framework endeavors to weave together the entrepreneurship, organizational, and (strategic) management literatures, while highlighting the critical roles of uncertainty, technological innovation, and organizational renewal for enterprise performance. This Element (a companion to *Dynamic Capabilities and Related Paradigms* in the same series) has shown how the framework relates to multiple antecedents in management and economics. While I argue that the dynamic capabilities framework encompasses these legacy concepts, it is more than a mere compendium.

Transaction costs, for example, are an important analytic concept from economics that can shed light on why a firm or ecosystem is structured in a particular way, and why it may need to be restructured. But, when considered as part of the dynamic capabilities framework, the analysis of transaction costs can be recognized as part of a more complex calculation that also evaluates the impact of various structural arrangements on production costs and on the potential for innovation.

The dynamic capabilities framework can also serve as the stepstool for the economic theory of the firm. It's vital for scholars to get the fundamentals right if they are to build and promote theories relevant to business and policy communities.

A commonsense notion of a firm's capabilities has always existed, but the concept of organizational capabilities as a subject of study is relatively recent, in academic terms. As mentioned in Section 2.3.2 on "Evolutionary routines," a version of organizational capabilities emerged in evolutionary economics in the 1980s (Teece, 2023c). However, the development of this early iteration was handicapped by explicitly placing managers at the mercy of inertia-bound organizational routines. The dynamic capabilities framework takes a broader, system-level view, arguing that, with the appropriate organizational culture and leadership by entrepreneurial managers, the inherent inertia of routines can be overcome.

When our original dynamic capabilities working paper appeared in 1990 (Teece, Pisano, and Shuen, 1990), there was no theory of capabilities in the management literature, much less of dynamic capabilities.[23] Since that time, perhaps in part because of my own work, along with important contributions by my original coauthors and by Connie Helfat, Peter Murmann, Sid Winter, and many others, considerable progress has been made.

There is now a large and still expanding literature on organizational capabilities. Whereas earlier research focused on the identification and evolution of capabilities (e.g., Helfat and Peteraf, 2003), recent studies are more likely to analyze specific capabilities, such as those for environmental sustainability or for digital transformation, and how they impact performance.

As this Element has attempted to show, dynamic capabilities provide the core of a capabilities-based theory of the firm. Complex managerial decisions, reduced in other theories of the firm to binary choices such as make or buy, are a primary focus of a firm's dynamic capabilities. The quality of top management decision making determines whether the firm's dynamic capabilities are weak or strong. The accumulated – and curated – legacy of past managerial decisions and the strategic vision and leadership of current management are what makes each firm unique. In other words, a (dynamic) capabilities-based theory can account for interfirm distinctiveness, unlike the older economic theories of the firm discussed in Section 3.2. An understanding of dynamic capabilities is therefore critical to a proper understanding of firms as they exist in the real world.

I ruminated on future directions for capabilities-based research in strategic management in the conclusion to *Dynamic Capabilities and Related Paradigms*. Here I'll add that, as each new concept arises in strategic management and the economics of the firm, it should be integrated and located in some wider theoretical framework such as dynamic capabilities in order to help students and decision makers understand its broader context and constraints. Continued deepening of a capabilities-based economic theory of the firm will pay dividends by facilitating the inclusion of capabilities in economic modeling and policy making. Without a proper theoretical grasp of capabilities, including dynamic capabilities, policy decisions are more likely to cause harms, such as undermining innovation.

---

[23] Capabilities thinking was perhaps in the air at the time; "The Core Competence of the Corporation" (Prahalad and Hamel, 1990) was published the same year. Core competencies are defined as "the collective learning in the organization, especially how to coordinate diverse production skills and integrate multiple streams of technologies" – a definition that captures certain aspects of dynamic capabilities, at least on the value creation side. However, the core competence approach, despite its initial embrace by large corporations, proved unreliable to implement and lacked any guidance for its application in a firm's specific business situation (Schaupp and Virkkunen, 2017).

References

Acemoglu, D., Akcigit, U., & Celik, M. A. (2022). Radical and incremental innovation: The roles of firms, managers, and innovators. *American Economic Journal: Macroeconomics, 14*(3), 199–249.

Aghion, P., & Tirole, J. (1997). Formal and real authority in organizations. *Journal of Political Economy, 105*(1), 1–29.

Alchian, A. A., & Demsetz, H. (1972). Production, information costs, and economic organization. *American Economic Review, 62*(5), 777–795.

Amadeo, R. (2023). App founder quits Google, says company doesn't serve users anymore. *Ars Technica.* https://arstechnica.com/gadgets/2023/02/app-founder-quits-google-says-company-doesnt-serve-users-anymore/.

Armour, H. O., & Teece, D. J. (1980). Vertical integration and technological innovation. *Review of Economics and Statistics, 62*(3), 470–474.

Arthur, W. B. (2021). Foundations of complexity economics. *Nature Reviews Physics, 3*(2), 136–145.

Augier, M., & Teece, D. J. (2008). Strategy as evolution with design: The foundations of dynamic capabilities and the role of managers in the economic system. *Organization Studies, 29*(8–9), 1187–1208.

Augier, M., & Teece, D. J. (2009). Dynamic capabilities and the role of managers in business strategy and economic performance. *Organization Science, 20*(2), 410–421.

Barnard, C. I. (1938). *The Functions of the Executive.* Cambridge, MA: Harvard University Press.

Barney, J. B. (1991). Firm resources and sustained competitive advantage. *Journal of Management, 17*(1), 99–120.

Baumol, W. J. (1968). Entrepreneurship in economic theory. *American Economic Review, 58*(2), 64–71.

Baumol, W. J. (2010). *The Microtheory of Innovative Entrepreneurship.* Princeton, NJ: Princeton University Press.

Benner, M. J., & Tushman, M. L. (2003). Exploitation, exploration, and process management: The productivity dilemma revisited. *Academy of Management Review, 28*(2), 238–256.

Bertrand, M., & Schoar, A. (2003). Managing with style: The effect of managers on firm policies. *Quarterly Journal of Economics, 118*(4), 1169–1208.

Bingham, C. B. (2009). Oscillating improvisation: How entrepreneurial firms create success in foreign market entries over time. *Strategic Entrepreneurship Journal, 3*(4), 321–345.

Bingham, C. B., & Eisenhardt, K. M. (2011). Rational heuristics: The "simple rules" that strategists learn from process experience. *Strategic Management Journal*, *32*(13), 1437–1464.

Bingham, C. B., Eisenhardt, K. M., & Furr, N. R. (2007). What makes a process a capability? Heuristics, strategy, and effective capture of opportunities. *Strategic Entrepreneurship Journal*, *1*(1–2), 27–47.

Bloom, N. (2017). Corporations in the age of inequality. *Harvard Business Review*. hbr.org/cover-story/2017/03/corporations-in-the-age-of-inequality (accessed April 20, 2017).

Bloom, N., Genakos, C., Sadun, R., & Van Reenen, J. (2012). Management practices across firms and countries. *Academy of Management Perspectives*, *26*(1), 12–33.

Boudreaux, D. J., & Holcombe, R. G. (1989). The Coasian and Knightian theories of the firm. *Managerial and Decision Economics*, *10*(2), 147–154.

Boulding, K. E. (1956). General systems theory – the skeleton of science. *Management Science*, *2*(3), 197–208.

Boulding, K. E. (1984). The fallacy of trends: On living with unpredictability. *National Forum*, *64*(3), 19.

Bourgeois, L. J., & Eisenhardt, K. M. (1988). Strategic decision-process in high-velocity environments: Four cases in the microcomputer industry. *Management Science*, *34*(7), 816–835.

Bresnahan, T. F. (1992). Sutton's sunk costs and market structure: Price competition, advertising, and the evolution of concentration. *RAND Journal of Economics*, *23*(1), 137–152.

Bresnahan, T. F., & Trajtenberg, M. (1995). General purpose technologies: "Engines of growth?" *Journal of Econometrics*, *65*(1), 83–108.

Brown, S. L., & Eisenhardt, K. M. (1997). The art of continuous change: Linking complexity theory and time-paced evolution in relentlessly shifting organizations. *Administrative Science Quarterly*, *42*(1), 1–34.

Burgelman, R. A. (1994). Fading memories: A process theory of strategic business exit in dynamic environments. *Administrative Science Quarterly*, *39*(1), 24–56.

Casson, M. (2005). Entrepreneurship and the theory of the firm. *Journal of Economic Behavior & Organization*, *58*(2), 327–348.

Chesbrough, H. W., & Teece, D. J. (1996). When is virtual virtuous? Organizing for innovation. *Harvard Business Review*, *74*(1), 65–72.

Clements, M. T. (2004). Direct and indirect network effects: Are they equivalent? *International Journal of Industrial Organization*, *22*(5), 633–645.

Coase, R. H. (1937). The nature of the firm. *Economica*, *4*(16), 386–405.

Coase, R., & Wang, N. (2012). Saving economics from the economists. *Harvard Business Review*, *90*(12), 36.

Cohen, W. M., & Levinthal, D. A. (1989). Innovation and learning: The two faces of R & D. *Economic Journal*, *99*(397), 569–596.

Cohen, W. M., & Levinthal, D. A. (1990). Absorptive capacity: A new perspective on learning and innovation. *Administrative Science Quarterly*, *35*(1), 128–152.

Cole, S. (2013). Apple's iPod continues to lead an ever-shrinking market of portable media players. *appleinsider.com*, December 19. appleinsider.com/articles/13/12/19/apples-ipod-continues-to-lead-an-ever-shrinking-market-of-portable-media-players (accessed February 2, 2019).

Courtney, H., Kirkland, J., & Viguerie, P. (1997). Strategy under uncertainty. *Harvard Business Review*, *75*(6), 67–79.

Cuofano, G. (2023). What is the Teece model? *FourWeekMBA*, https://fourweekmba.com/teece-model/.

Cyert, R. M., & March, J. G. (1963). *A Behavioral Theory of the Firm*. Englewood Cliffs, NJ: Prentice-Hall.

Davis, J. G. (2016). Growth share matrix. In M. Augier, & D. Teece (Eds.), *The Palgrave Encyclopedia of Strategic Management*. London: Palgrave Macmillan. https://doi.org/10.1057/978-1-349-94848-2_692-1.

De Figueiredo, J. M., & Teece, D. J. (1996). Mitigating procurement hazards in the context of innovation. *Industrial and Corporate Change*, *5*(2), 537–559.

Demsetz, H. (1976). Economics as a guide to antitrust regulation. *Journal of Law and Economics*, *19*(2), 371–384.

Denrell, J., Fang, C., & Winter, S. G. (2003). The economics of strategic opportunity. *Strategic Management Journal*, *24*(10), 977–990.

Dessein, W., & Santos, T. (2006). Adaptive organizations. *Journal of Political Economy*, *114*(5), 956–995.

Di Stefano, G., Peteraf, M., & Verona, G. (2010). Dynamic capabilities deconstructed: A bibliographic investigation into the origins, development, and future directions of the research domain. *Industrial and Corporate Change*, *19*(4), 1187–1204.

Durand, R., Grant, R. M., & Madsen, T. L. (2017). The expanding domain of strategic management research and the quest for integration. *Strategic Management Journal*, *38*(1), 4–16.

Edgeworth, F. Y. (1897). Teoria pura del monopolio. *Giornale degli Economisti*, *15*, 13–31. Translated as "The pure theory of monopoly" in F. Y. Edgeworth (1925). *Papers Relating to Political Economy*, *vol. I*. London: Macmillan, 111–142.

Eisenhardt, K. M., & Martin, J. A. (2000). Dynamic capabilities: What are they? *Strategic Management Journal, 21*(10–11), 1105–1121.

Eisenhardt, K. M., & Piezunka, H. (2011). Complexity theory and corporate strategy. In P. Allen, S. Maguire, & B. McKelvey (Eds.), *The SAGE Handbook of Complexity and Management*. Los Angeles, CA: SAGE, 506–523.

Eisenhardt, K. M., & Sull, D. N. (2001). Strategy as simple rules. *Harvard Business Review, 79*(1), 106–116.

Eisenhardt, K. M., & Tabrizi, B. N. (1995). Accelerating adaptive processes: Product innovation in the global computer industry. *Administrative Science Quarterly, 40*, 84–110.

Follett, M. P. (1926). The psychological foundations: The giving of orders. In H. C. Metcalf (Ed.), *Scientific Foundations of Business Administration*. Baltimore, MD: The Williams & Wilkins, 132–149.

Friebel, G., & Raith, M. (2010). Resource allocation and organizational form. *American Economic Journal: Microeconomics, 2*(2), 1–33.

Garicano, L. (2000). Hierarchies and the organization of knowledge in production. *Journal of Political Economy, 108*(5), 874–904.

Garicano, L., & Rossi-Hansberg, E. (2012). Organizing growth. *Journal of Economic Theory, 147*(2), 623–656.

Geissler, C., & Krys, C. (2013). The challenges of strategic management in the twenty-first century. In B. Schwenker & T. Wulf (Eds.), *Scenario-Based Strategic Planning: Developing Strategies in an Uncertain World*. Wiesbaden: Springer Gabler, 21–41.

Gibbons, R. (2005). Four formal(izable) theories of the firm? *Journal of Economic Behavior & Organization, 58*(2), 200–245.

Golder, P. N. (2000). Historical method in marketing research with new evidence on long-term market share stability. *Journal of Marketing Research, 37*(2), 156–172.

Grant, R. M. (1996). Toward a knowledge-based theory of the firm. *Strategic Management Journal, 17*(S2), 109–122.

Grant, R., & Phene, A. (2022). The knowledge based view and global strategy: Past impact and future potential. *Global Strategy Journal, 12*(1), 3–30.

Gratton, L., & Ghoshal, S. (2005). Beyond best practice. *MIT Sloan Management Review, 46*(3), 49–57.

Grindley, P. C., & Teece, D. J. (1997). Managing intellectual capital: Licensing and cross-licensing in semiconductors and electronics. *California Management Review, 39*(2), 8–41.

Hague, D. C. (1958). Alfred Marshall and the competitive firm. *Economic Journal, 68*(272), 673–690.

Hague, P. (2019). Teece model – Profiting from innovation. *B2B Frameworks*, www.b2bframeworks.com/profiting-from-innovation.

Hamel, G., & Zanini, M. (2022). Fixing bureaucracy requires more than a month-long sprint. Here's why. *Fast Company*, www.fastcompany.com/90789977/fixing-bureaucracy-requires-more-than-a-month-long-sprint-heres-why.

Hannan, M. T., & Freeman, J. (1977). The population ecology of organizations. *American Journal of Sociology, 82*(5), 929–964.

Hart, O. (2011). Thinking about the firm: A review of Daniel Spulber's the Theory of the Firm. *Journal of Economic Literature, 49*(1), 101–113.

Hart, O., & Moore, J. (1990). Property rights and the nature of the firm. *Journal of Political Economy, 98*(6), 1119–1158.

Hastings, R., & Meyer, E. (2020). *No Rules Rules: Netflix and the Culture of Reinvention*. New York: Penguin Press.

Helfat, C. E., & Peteraf, M. A. (2003). The dynamic resource-based view: Capability lifecycles. *Strategic Management Journal, 24*(10), 997–1010.

Helfat, C. E., & Teece, D. J. (1987). Vertical integration and risk reduction. *Journal of Law, Economics, and Organization, 3*(1), 47–67.

Helpman, E. (Ed.) (1998). *General Purpose Technologies and Economic Growth*. Cambridge, MA: MIT Press.

Henderson, B. D. (1970). The product portfolio. *Boston Consulting Group Perspective, 66*. www.bcg.com/publications/1970/strategy-the-product-portfolio.

Hilzenrath, D. S. (1998). Merck offers refund if Zocor doesn't work; cholesterol drug has lost market lead. *Washington Post*, November 6, p. F03.

Hitt, M. A., Keats, B. W., & DeMarie, S. M. (1998). Navigating in the new competitive landscape: Building strategic flexibility and competitive advantage in the 21st century. *Academy of Management Perspectives, 12*(4), 22–42.

Holmstrom, B., & Milgrom, P. (1994). The firm as an incentive system. *American Economic Review, 84*(4), 972–991.

Ifandoudas, P., & Chapman, R. (2009). A practical approach to achieving agility–a theory of constraints perspective. *Production Planning & Control, 20*(8), 691–702.

Inderst, R., & Klein, M. (2007). Innovation, endogenous overinvestment, and incentive pay. *RAND Journal of Economics, 38*(4), 881–904.

Jacobides, M. G. (2019). In the ecosystem economy, what's your strategy? *Harvard Business Review, 97*(5), 128–137.

Jacobides, M. G., Knudsen, T., & Augier, M. (2006). Benefiting from innovation: Value creation, value appropriation and the role of industry architectures. *Research Policy, 35*(8), 1200–1221.

Janeway, W. H. (2012). *Doing Capitalism in the Innovation Economy: Markets, Speculation and the State.* Cambridge: Cambridge University Press.

Jensen, M. C., & Meckling, W. H. (1976). Theory of the firm: Managerial behavior, agency costs and ownership structure. *Journal of Financial Economics, 3*(4), 305–360.

Jones, B. (2012). Comment on "generality, recombination, and reuse." In J. Lerner & S. Stern (Eds.), *The Rate and Direction of Inventive Activity Revisited.* Chicago, IL: University of Chicago Press, 656–661.

Kay, N. M., Leih, S., & Teece, D. J. (2018). The role of emergence in dynamic capabilities: A restatement of the framework and some possibilities for future research. *Industrial and Corporate Change, 27*(4), 623–638.

Keynes, J. M. (1936). *The General Theory of Employment, Interest and Money.* London: Macmillan.

Kirzner, I. M. (1985). *Discovery and the Capitalist Process.* Chicago, IL: University of Chicago Press.

Kirzner, I. M. (1997). Entrepreneurial discovery and the competitive market process: An Austrian approach. *Journal of Economic Literature, 35*(1), 60–85.

Klemperer, P. (2002). What really matters in auction design. *Journal of Economic Perspectives, 16*(1), 169–189.

Knight, F. H. (1921). *Risk, Uncertainty, and Profit.* New York: Harper.

Koopmans, T. C. (1957). *Three Essays on the State of Economic Science.* New York: McGraw-Hill.

Kraaijenbrink, J., Spender, J. C., & Groen, A. J. (2010). The resource-based view: A review and assessment of its critiques. *Journal of Management, 36*(1), 349–372.

Lane, P. J., & Lubatkin, M. (1998). Relative absorptive capacity and interorganizational learning. *Strategic Management Journal, 19*(5), 461–477.

Langlois, R. N. (1992). Transaction-cost economics in real time. *Industrial and Corporate Change, 1*(1), 99–127.

Lazonick, W., & Shin, J. S. (2020). *Predatory Value Extraction: How the Looting of the Business Corporation Became the US Norm and How Sustainable Prosperity Can Be Restored.* Oxford: Oxford University Press.

Lev, B., & Radhakrishnan, S. (2005). The valuation of organization capital. In C. Corrado, J. Haltiwanger, & D. Sichel (Eds.), *Measuring Capital in the New Economy.* Chicago, IL: University of Chicago Press, 73–110.

Levy, D. (1994). Chaos theory and strategy: Theory, application, and managerial implications. *Strategic Management Journal*, *15*(S2), 167–178.

Levy, D. L. (2000). Applications and limitations of complexity theory in organization theory and strategy. In J. Rabin, G. J. Miller, & W. B. Hildreth (Eds.), *Handbook of Strategic Management*. New York: Marcel Dekker, 67–87.

Li, H. L., & Tang, M. J. (2010). Vertical integration and innovative performance: The effects of external knowledge sourcing modes. *Technovation*, *30* (7–8), 401–410.

Lim, K. (2009). The many faces of absorptive capacity: Spillovers of copper interconnect technology for semiconductor chips. *Industrial and Corporate Change*, *18*(6), 1249–1284.

Linden, G., & Teece, D. J. (2018). Conglomerates. In M. Augier & D. J. Teece (Eds.), *The Palgrave Encyclopedia of Strategic Management*. London: Palgrave Macmillan. https://doi.org/10.1057/978-1-137-00772-8_405.

Lippman, S. A., & Rumelt, R. P. (1982). Uncertain imitability: An analysis of interfirm differences in efficiency under competition. *Bell Journal of Economics*, *13*(2), 418–438.

Lovallo, D., Brown, A. L., Teece, D. J., & Bardolet, D. (2020). Resource reallocation capabilities in internal capital markets: The value of overcoming inertia. *Strategic Management Journal*, *41*(8), 1365–1380.

Malmgren, H. B. (1961). Information, expectations and the theory of the firm. *Quarterly Journal of Economics*, *75*(3), 399–421.

March, J. G. (1991). Exploration and exploitation in organizational learning. *Organization Science*, *2*(1), 71–87.

Marshall, A. (1898). *Principles of Economics, 4th edition*. London: MacMillan and Co.

Marshall, A. (1919). *Industry and Trade*. London: Macmillan.

Marshall, A. (1920). *Principles of Economics (8th ed.)*. London: Macmillan.

Marx, K., & Engels, F. (1848/1906). *Manifesto of the Communist Party*. Translated by Samuel Moore. Chicago, IL: C. H. Kerr.

Matsusaka, J. G. (2001). Corporate diversification, value maximization, and organizational capabilities. *Journal of Business*, *74*(3), 409–431.

Mayo, E. (1933). *The Human Problems of an Industrial Civilization*. New York: Macmillan.

Mercer LLC. (2012). The congruence model: A roadmap for understanding organizational performance. www.academia.edu/26617289/Delta_Mercer_Congruence_Model (accessed December 19, 2023).

Michaels, D., & Sanders, P. (2009). Dreamliner production gets closer monitoring. *Wall Street Journal*, October 8. www.wsj.com/articles/SB125486824367569007.

Nadler, D. A., & Tushman, M. L. (1980). A model for diagnosing organizational behavior. *Organizational Dynamics*, *9*(2), 35–51.

Nelson, R. R., & Winter, S. G. (1982). *An Evolutionary Theory of Economic Change*. Cambridge, MA: Belknap Press.

Nicita, A., & Vatiero, M. (2014). Dixit versus Williamson: The "fundamental transformation" reconsidered. *European Journal of Law and Economics*, *37*, 439–453.

Nonaka, I. (1988). Toward middle-up-down management: Accelerating information creation. *MIT Sloan Management Review*, *29*(3), 9–18.

North, M. J., & Macal, C. M. (2007). *Managing Business Complexity: Discovering Strategic Solutions with Agent-Based Modeling and Simulation*. Oxford: Oxford University Press.

O'Reilly, C. A., & Tushman, M. L. (2004). The ambidextrous organization. *Harvard Business Review*, *82*(4), 74–81.

O'Reilly, C. A., & Tushman, M. L. (2013). Organizational ambidexterity: Past, present, and future. *Academy of Management Perspectives*, *27*(4), 324–338.

Penrose, E. T. (1959). *Theory of the Growth of the Firm*. Oxford: Blackwell.

Pesciarelli, E. (1988). Smith, Bentham and the development of contrasting ideas on entrepreneurship. University of Ancona, Department of Economics. docs.dises.univpm.it/web/quaderni/pdf/011.pdf (accessed March 12, 2023).

Pitelis, C. N., & Teece, D. J. (2009). The (new) nature and essence of the firm. *European Management Review*, *6*(1), 5–15.

Porter, M. E. (1979). The structure within industries and companies' performance. *Review of Economics and Statistics*, *61*(2), 214–227.

Pisano, G. P., & Teece, D. J. (2007). How to capture value from innovation: Shaping intellectual property and industry architecture. *California Management Review*, *50*(1), 278–296.

Prahalad, C. K., & Hamel, G. (1990). The core competence of the corporation. *Harvard Business Review*, *68*(3), 79–91.

Prescott, E. C., & Visscher, M. (1980). Organization capital. *Journal of Political Economy*, *88*(3), 446–461.

PwC. (2024). A CFO imperative: Smart resource reallocation. www.pwc.com/gx/en/issues/c-suite-insights/the-leadership-agenda/a-cfo-imperative-smart-resource-allocation.html (accessed March 8, 2024).

Richardson, G. (1960). *Information and Investment*. London: Oxford University Press.

Richardson, G. (1972). The organisation of industry. *Economic Journal, 82*(326), 883–896.

Rosenberg, N. (1979). Technological interdependence in the American economy. *Technology and Culture, 20*(1), 25–50.

Rosenberg, N. (1982). *Inside the Black Box: Technology and Economics*. New York: Cambridge University Press.

Rubin, P. H. (1973). The expansion of firms. *Journal of Political Economy, 81* (4), 936–949.

Rule, J. N. (2013). A symbiotic relationship: The OODA loop, intuition, and strategic thought. Carlisle Barracks, PA: U.S. Army War College. apps.dtic.mil/sti/pdfs/ADA590672.pdf (accessed November 1, 2024).

Rumelt, R. (1984). Towards a strategic theory of the firm. In R. B. Lamb (Ed.), *Competitive Strategic Management*. Englewood Cliffs, NJ: Prentice-Hall, 556–570.

Rumelt, R. P. (1987). Theory, strategy, and entrepreneurship. In D. J. Teece (Ed.), *The Competitive Challenge: Strategies for Industrial Innovation and Renewal*. Cambridge, MA: Ballinger, 137–158.

Rumelt, R. P., Schendel, D., & Teece, D. J. (1991). Strategic management and economics. *Strategic Management Journal, 12*(S2), 5–29.

Rumelt, R. (2011). *Good Strategy/Bad Strategy: The Difference and Why It Matters*. New York: Crown Business.

Russell, B. (1946/1972). *The History of Western Philosophy*. New York: Simon Schuster.

Sautet, F. E. (2000). *An Entrepreneurial Theory of the Firm*. London: Routledge.

Schaupp, M., & Virkkunen, J. (2017). Why a management concept fails to support managers' work: The case of the "core competence of a corporation." *Management Learning, 48*(1), 97–109.

Schneider, M., & Somers, M. (2006). Organizations as complex adaptive systems: Implications of complexity theory for leadership research. *Leadership Quarterly, 17*(4), 351–365.

Schoemaker, P. J., Heaton, S., & Teece, D. (2018). Innovation, dynamic capabilities, and leadership. *California Management Review, 61*(1), 15–42.

Schumpeter, J. A. (1934). *The Theory of Economic Development*. Cambridge, MA: Harvard University Press.

Schumpeter, J. A. (1942). *Capitalism, Socialism and Democracy*. New York: Harper and Brothers.

Scocco, D. (2006). The Teece model. *Innovation Zen*, http://innovationzen.com/blog/2006/08/24/innovation-management-theory-part-5/.

Sellers, P., & Kirkpatrick, D. (1993). Can this man save IBM? *Fortune, 127*(8), April 19, 63–67.

Sidak, J. G., & Teece, D. J. (2009). Dynamic competition in antitrust law. *Journal of Competition Law and Economics*, *5*(4), 581–631.

Simon, H. A. (1957). *Models of Man: Social and Rational*. New York: Wiley.

Somaya, D., & Teece, D. J. (2006). Patents, licensing and entrepreneurship: Effectuating innovation in multi-invention contexts. In E. Sheshinski, R. J. Strom, & W. J. Baumol (Eds.), *Entrepreneurship, Innovation, and the Growth of Free-Market Economies*. Princeton, NJ: Princeton University Press, 185–212.

Song, J., Lee, K., & Khanna, T. (2016). Dynamic capabilities at Samsung: Optimizing internal co-opetition. *California Management Review*, *58*(4), 118–140.

Spender, J. C. (1994). Organizational knowledge, collective practice and Penrose rents. *International Business Review*, *3*(4), 353–367.

Spender, J. C. (1996). Making knowledge the basis of a dynamic theory of the firm. *Strategic Management Journal*, *17*(S2), 45–62.

Stein, J. C. (2002). Information production and capital allocation: Decentralized versus hierarchical firms. *Journal of Finance*, *57*(5), 1891–1921.

Stigler, G. (1939). Production and distribution in the short run. *Journal of Political Economy*, *47*(3), 305–327.

Sull, D., & Eisenhardt, K. M. (2012). Simple rules for a complex world. *Harvard Business Review*, *90*(9), 68–74.

Sutton, J. (2002). Rich trades, scarce capabilities: Industrial development revisited. *Economic and Social Review*, *33*(1), 1–22.

Sutton, J. (2012). *Competing in Capabilities: The Globalization Process*. Oxford: Oxford University Press.

Taleb, N. N. (2007). *The Black Swan: The Impact of the Highlight Improbable*. New York: Random House.

Taylor, F. W. (1911). *The Principles of Scientific Management*. New York: Harper & Brothers.

Teece, D. J. (1980). Economies of scope and the scope of the enterprise. *Journal of Economic Behavior & Organization*, *1*(3), 223–247.

Teece, D. J. (1981). The market for know-how and the efficient international transfer of technology. *Annals of the Academy of Political and Social Science*, *458*(1), 81–96.

Teece, D. J. (1982). Towards an economic theory of the multiproduct firm. *Journal of Economic Behavior & Organization*, *3*(1), 39–63.

Teece, D. J. (1984). Economic analysis and strategic management. *California Management Review*, *26*(3), 87–110.

Teece, D. J. (1986). Profiting from technological innovation: Implications for integration, collaboration, licensing and public policy. *Research Policy, 15* (6), 285–305.

Teece, D. J. (1990). Structure and organization of the natural gas industry: Differences between the United States and the Federal Republic of Germany and implications for the carrier status of pipelines. *Energy Journal, 11*(3), 1–35.

Teece, D. J. (2006). Reflections on "profiting from innovation." *Research Policy, 35*(8), 1131–1146.

Teece, D. J. (2007). Explicating dynamic capabilities: The nature and micro-foundations of (sustainable) enterprise performance. *Strategic Management Journal, 28*(13), 1319–1350.

Teece, D. J. (2010a). Business models, business strategy and innovation. *Long Range Planning, 43*(2–3), 172–194.

Teece, D. J. (2010b). Technological innovation and the theory of the firm: The role of enterprise-level knowledge, complementarities, and (dynamic) capabilities. In N. Rosenberg & B. H. Hall (Eds.), *Handbook of the Economics of Innovation, Vol.1*. Oxford: North-Holland, 679–730.

Teece, D. J. (2011a). Achieving integration of the business school curriculum using the dynamic capabilities framework. *Journal of Management Development, 30* (5), 499–518.

Teece, D. J. (2011b). Human capital, capabilities and the firm: Literati, numerati, and entrepreneurs in the 21st-century enterprise. In A. Burton-Jones & J.-C. Spender (Eds.), *The Oxford Handbook of Human Capital*. Oxford: Oxford University Press, 527–562.

Teece, D. J. (2012a). Dynamic capabilities: Routines versus entrepreneurial action. *Journal of Management Studies, 49*(8), 1395–1401.

Teece, D. J. (2012b). Next-generation competition: New concepts for understanding how innovation shapes competition and policy in the digital economy. *Journal of Law, Economics, and Policy, 9*(1), 97–118.

Teece, D. J. (2015). Intangible assets and a theory of heterogeneous firms. In A. Bounfour & T. Miyagawa (Eds.), *Intangibles, Market Failure and Innovation Performance*. New York: Springer, 217–239.

Teece, D. J. (2016a). Dynamic capabilities and entrepreneurial management in large organizations: Toward a theory of the (entrepreneurial) firm. *European Economic Review, 86*, 202–216.

Teece, D. J. (2016b). Business ecosystem. In M. Augier & D. J. Teece (Eds.), *The Palgrave Encyclopedia of Strategic Management*. London: Palgrave Macmillan. https://doi.org/10.1057/978-1-349-94848-2_724-1.

Teece, D. J. (2017). Towards a capability theory of (innovating) firms: implications for management and policy. *Cambridge Journal of Economics*, *41*(3), 693–720.

Teece, D. J. (2018a). Dynamic capabilities as (workable) management systems theory. *Journal of Management & Organization*, *24*(3), 359–368.

Teece, D. J. (2018b). Profiting from innovation in the digital economy: Enabling technologies, standards, and licensing models in the wireless world. *Research Policy*, *47*(8), 1367–1387.

Teece, D. J. (2018c). Capability development. In M. Augier & D. J. Teece (Eds.), *The Palgrave Encyclopedia of Strategic Management*. London: Palgrave Macmillan, 192–194. https://doi.org/10.1057/978-1-137-00772-8_572.

Teece, D. J. (2019a). Strategic renewal and dynamic capabilities: Managing uncertainty, irreversibilities, and congruence. In A. Tuncdogan, A. Lindgreen, F. Van Den Bosch, & H. Volberda (Eds.), *Strategic Renewal: Core Concepts, Antecedents, and Micro Foundations*. London: Routledge, 21–51.

Teece, D. J. (2019b). A capability theory of the firm: An economics and (strategic) management perspective. *New Zealand Economic Papers*, *53*(1), 1–43.

Teece, D. J. (2023a). Big tech and strategic management: How management scholars can inform competition policy. *Academy of Management Perspectives*, *37*(1), 1–15.

Teece, D. J. (2023b). The dynamic competition paradigm: Insights and implications. *Columbia Business Law Review*, *2023*(1), 373–461.

Teece, D. J. (2023c). Evolutionary economics, routines, and dynamic capabilities. In R. Nelson, K. Dopfer, J. Potts, & A. Pyka (Eds.), *The Handbook of Evolutionary Economics*. London: Routledge, 197–214.

Teece, D. J. (2025). The multinational enterprise, capabilities, and digitalization: governance and growth with world disorder. *Journal of International Business Studies*, *56*, 7–22.

Teece, D., Peteraf, M., & Leih, S. (2016). Dynamic capabilities and organizational agility: Risk, uncertainty, and strategy in the innovation economy. *California Management Review*, *58*(4), 13–35.

Teece, D. J., Pisano, G., & Shuen, A. (1990). Firm capabilities, resources, and the concept of strategy. CCC Working Paper 90–8, Center for Research in Management. University of California.

Teece, D. J., Pisano, G., & Shuen, A. (1997). Dynamic capabilities and strategic management. *Strategic Management Journal*, *18*(7), 509–533.

References

Teece, D. J., Rumelt, R., Dosi, G., & Winter, S. (1994). Understanding corporate coherence: Theory and evidence. *Journal of Economic Behavior & Organization, 23*(1), 1–30.

Teece, D. J., & Winter, S. G. (1984). The limits of neoclassical theory in management education. *American Economic Review, 74*(2), 116–121.

Thiel, P. (2014). Lecture 5: Business strategy and monopoly theory. *Genius.com*. genius.com/Peter-thiel-lecture-5-business-strategy-and-monopoly-theory-annotated (accessed February 14, 2017).

Tushman, M. L., & Anderson, P. (1986). Technological discontinuities and organizational environments. *Administrative Science Quarterly, 31*(3), 439–465.

Tushman, M. L., & O'Reilly, C. A. (1996). The ambidextrous organization: Managing evolutionary and revolutionary change. *California Management Review, 38*, 1–23.

Wakabayashi, D. (2021). Google executives see cracks in their company's success. *New York Times*, www.nytimes.com/2021/06/21/technology/sundar-pichai-google.html.

Watts, B., & Augier, M. (2022). John Boyd on competition and conflict. *Comparative Strategy, 41*(3), 233–260.

Wernerfelt, B. (1984). A resource-based view of the firm. *Strategic Management Journal, 5*(2), 171–180.

Wilden, R., Gudergan, S. P., Nielsen, B. B., & Lings, I. (2013). Dynamic capabilities and performance: Strategy, structure and environment. *Long Range Planning, 46*(1–2), 72–96.

Williamson, O. E. (1975). *Markets and Hierarchies*. New York: Free Press.

Williamson, O. E. (1985a). *The Economic Institutions of Capitalism*. New York: Free Press.

Williamson, O. E. (1985b). Assessing contract. *The Journal of Law, Economics, and Organization, 1*(1), 177–208.

Williamson, O. E. (1993). The evolving science of organization. *Journal of Institutional and Theoretical Economics, 149*(1), 36–63.

Winter, S. G. (2006). The logic of appropriability: From Schumpeter to Arrow to Teece. *Research Policy, 35*(8), 1100–1106.

Worley, C. G., Williams, T., & Lawler, E. E. (2014). *The Agility Factor: Building Adaptable Organizations for Superior Performance*. San Francisco, CA: Jossey-Bass.

Zahra, S. A., & George, G. (2002). Absorptive capacity: A review, reconceptualization, and extension. *Academy of Management Review, 27*(2), 185–203.

Acknowledgment

The author thanks Greg Linden and two reviewers for very helpful comments and assistance.

Cambridge Elements

Business Strategy

J.-C. Spender
Kozminski University

J.-C. Spender is a research Professor, Kozminski University. He has been active in the business strategy field since 1971 and is the author or co-author of 7 books and numerous papers. His principal academic interest is in knowledge-based theories of the private sector firm, and managing them.

Advisory Board

Jay Barney, *Eccles School of Business, The University of Utah*
Stewart Clegg, *University of Technology, Sydney*
Thomas Durand, *Conservatoire National des Arts et Métiers, Paris*
CT Foo, *Independent Scholar, Singapore*
Robert Grant, *Bocconi University, Milan*
Robin Holt, *Copenhagen Business School*
Paula Jarzabkowski, *Cass School, City University, London*
Naga Lakshmi Damaraju, *Indian School of Business*
Marjorie Lyles, *Kelley School of Business, Indiana University*
Joseph T. Mahoney, *College of Business, University of Illinois at Urbana-Champaign*
Nicolai Foss, *Bocconi University, Milan*
Andreas Scherer, *University of Zurich*
Deepak Somaya, *College of Business, University of Illinois at Urbana-Champaign*
Eduard van Gelderen, *Chief Investment Officer, APG, Amsterdam*

About the Series

Business strategy's reach is vast, and important too since wherever there is business activity there is strategizing. As a field, strategy has a long history from medieval and colonial times to today's developed and developing economies. This series offers a place for interesting and illuminating research including industry and corporate studies, strategizing in service industries, the arts, the public sector, and the new forms of Internet-based commerce. It also covers today's expanding gamut of analytic techniques.

Cambridge Elements

Business Strategy

Elements in the Series

Business Model Innovation: Strategic and Organizational Issues for Established Firms
Constantinos Markides

Evolution of the Automobile Industry: A Capability-Architecture-Performance Approach
Takahiro Fujimoto

People Centric Innovation Ecosystem: Japanese Management and Practices
Yingying Zhang-Zhang and Takeo Kikkawa

Strategizing in the Polish Furniture Industry
Paulina Bednarz-Łuczewska

A Historical Review of Swedish Strategy Research and the Rigor-Relevance Gap
Thomas Kalling and Lars Bengtsson

Global Strategy in Our Age of Chaos: How Will the Multinational Firm Survive?
Stephen Tallman and Mitchell P. Koza

Strategizing With Institutional Theory
Harry Sminia

Effectuation: Rethinking Fundamental Concepts in the Social Sciences
Saras Sarasvathy

Behavioral Strategy: Exploring Microfoundations of Competitive Advantage
Nicolai J. Foss, Ambra Mazzelli and Libby Weber

Digital Assets: A Portfolio Perspective
Henrique Schneider

Diversification in the World of Data and AI
Gianvito Lanzolla and Constantinos Markides

Dynamic Capabilities: Foundational Concepts
David J. Teece

A full series listing is available at: www.cambridge.org/EBUS

For EU product safety concerns, contact us at Calle de José Abascal, 56–1°, 28003 Madrid, Spain or eugpsr@cambridge.org.

www.ingramcontent.com/pod-product-compliance
Ingram Content Group UK Ltd.
Pitfield, Milton Keynes, MK11 3LW, UK
UKHW022123060326
468743UK00020B/3500